MW01110042

Absence of Doubt

When the Search for Enlightenment STOPS

By Jill L. Warner

Including a conversation with

Gangaji

Copyright © 2003, 2004, 2005 by Jill L. Warner

All rights reserved. No part of this book shall be reproduced, stored in a retrieval system, or transmitted by any means – electronic, mechanical, photocopying, recording, or otherwise – without the written permission of the author.

Third Edition: 2005

Printed in Canada

ISBN 0-9748805-0-7

Book cover designed by Dori Friend
Final editing by Van English
Graphic image: Sun rising over the Earth from Space

For more information, please write to:

One Message Publishing
3451 Dry Creek Road
Ione, CA 95640

phone: 800-394-1961

"Know the Truth and the Truth will make you free."

- Jesus

ॐ

Bhagavan Sri Ramana Maharshi

ॐ

Dedication

This book is dedicated to Bhagavan Sri Ramana Maharshi and his beloved Arunachala. It is the Grace of his ancient teacher Arunachala and the endless Grace of Ramana, the Grace of God, as well as his beloved students and teachers, Papaji and Gangaji, who made this book possible. Ramana's courage to meet his own death created a gateway of light that has enabled thousands to become fully Self-realized. His light is eternal, his love is eternal, and his endless grace has removed my doubt forever.

Introduction

There was a time long ago when the ancient sages knew the secret path to enlightenment, known as the "great way." They understood that the "way" is the most direct route to freedom, open to anyone who has a strong desire to be free from suffering. Over the centuries, this path has been obscured by religious dogma, spiritual practice, beliefs, fear, uncertainty, and doubt. The dilemma in attempting to reveal this "way" to you is and always has been words themselves. There are Tibetan words, Zen words, Lakota words, Christian words, Hindu words, and New Age words, which all point to the living Truth that cannot be contained by any word. It is a Truth that lives within you. This is freedom itself.

For centuries this way was hidden from the average person, until a sixteen-year-old boy rediscovered it. This boy grew up to become Bhagavan Sri Ramana Maharshi, one of the greatest Saints whom India has ever known. What Ramana discovered represents the most radical and direct path for recognizing your own enlightenment. His discovery transcends all religions and eliminates the spiritual practices that are believed to be necessary to attain the state of enlightenment. It enables the average person to surpass all knowledge and experience a direct, unknowable recognition of the infinite peace, happiness, and freedom of enlightenment - for centuries believed to be reserved only for the most holy people. Through some unknowable grace, Ramana recognized the *essential question* that unlocks the mystery of this simple way, literally enabling anyone who is ready to take the deepest drink of Truth to recognize his or her own eternal freedom.

Whether you seek enlightenment or the peace that enlightenment promises, or more simply, if you are trying to put an end to your own suffering, it is here that your search can stop; it is here that your suffering can end. This book reveals the way to freedom by speaking simply and plainly, revealing the core meaning behind every aspect of what is known as the *essential context*. The *essential context* is made up of a group of key words that provide a context for seeing something that can only be seen by the heart. You have probably heard many of these words before, but without a clear definition of their meanings in the context of discovering the "great way" of enlightenment, they can cloud your mind with useless information. The *essential context* provides the core meaning behind words that point to a deeper Truth that no word or words can define. Each one of these words has the power to be a gateway or a barrier to freedom. Ultimately, it is up to you to decide.

To comprehend the ancient and divine meaning of the *essential context,* you must abandon your normal ways of understanding and instead, simply open. When you approach this book from this opening, with an open mind and heart, allowing yourself to let go of everything you think you know, you will be free to receive a transmission of Grace—mind to mind, heart to heart, core to core. It is an openness to receive what is already here, That which has always been here every moment of your life: your own enlightenment, the recognition that you are freedom itself. Even if you doubt that this is possible, it is here that you can discover the source of the doubter, giving you the ultimate gift of enlightenment: the complete and total *absence of doubt.*

The great awakening that enlightenment promises is occurring right here, right now, in this moment. Whether you know it or not, you are living in a time when the average person can recognize his or her own enlightenment known as *nirvana,* or freedom from suffering. The purpose of this book is to penetrate through to the very core of your being, to penetrate deep into your sacred heart, revealing the infinite depth of your own eternal freedom.

J. L. W.

Ego

Ego has been perceived as the greatest barrier to freedom. It has been seen as the great dark force, a personal nemesis that must be overcome. It has been recognized as the source of all negative emotions: Greed, jealousy, hatred, revenge, and suffering have all emerged from ego. From this recognition, a core belief has evolved in many spiritual communities. It is a deep belief that you must destroy your ego through spiritual practice, devotion, and prayer if you want to attain the coveted state of enlightenment. There is nothing wrong with spiritual practices, religion, devotion, or prayer; however, these spiritual communities and many seekers of Truth have failed to recognize that the desire to destroy ego *is* ego. Only ego cares about ego. Do you think God or pure consciousness is concerned about ego?

Having a clear definition of what ego is will help clarify the first aspect of the *essential context.* The core definition of ego is the thought "I." When the thought "I" emerges into your consciousness, there is a natural immediate separation from everyone and everything. From your initial "I" thought, many other thoughts emerge to support the belief that you are separate, that you have a unique identity. At its core, ego emerges from the primal "I" thought and evolves into the very deep belief in the idea, "I am this body" or "I am me."

Ego has three distinct aspects to it. There is a physical aspect (identification with the body), an emotional aspect (the feeling that "I am separate"), and a verbal or mental aspect (built on your history, experiences and desires that create the story of you as a unique and separate individual). These three aspects of ego work together to create the natural belief that you are separate from everyone and everything. This core belief is the root cause of all human suffering and is the primary reason that many spiritual communities believe that the destruction of the ego is necessary in order to attain the state of Self-realization or enlightenment, the freedom that you are seeking.

In Truth, your ego is a sacred gift; it is literally a gateway into the infinite. It becomes a barrier only when you think you are unique and separate from everyone. It transforms into a gateway when you turn your awareness toward the source of the primal "I" thought. When you become aware of the source of the ego, the gateway of pure consciousness opens by itself. There is no need of *doing* on your part!

Although understanding ego helps clarify what it is, understanding alone will not help you in your quest for freedom. To discover the freedom you are seeking, you must first understand why you think you are not free. Why are you not free? Who says you are not free? Or who says you *are* free? I invite you to take a moment right here, right now to contemplate these two questions: *Who says you are free? Who says you are <u>not</u> free?* You might notice a laundry list of things, events, people, and concepts that say you are free or not free. For now this is enough; simply notice.

Take a moment and contemplate these questions: *Who am I? Where am I going? What does my life mean?* Notice what is revealed: It might be a name, a job title, a desire, or a goal. All of these ideas create the story of you, which defines who you think you are and controls you either consciously or unconsciously. These concepts and ideas of who you are and where you are going are simply concepts and ideas, or a collection of thoughts.

When you are born you come into this world with no name, no clothes, no possessions, no idea of where you were or where you are going – no nothing. Then, someone gives you a name, clothes, a place to live. As time goes on, all you know about yourself is the identity that was given to you: *I am John; my parents are John and Kelly Smith; I live at 1920 Kenbar Court in McLean, Virginia; my phone number is 703-555-8091.* These identities create the context or *story* of you – your conditioned existence – which began the very moment you entered the world.

Naturally, you have a very deep belief that you are this person, this identity given at the time of birth. Over time this identity evolves into a super identity, a huge story proving that all the identities and experiences that you have created are really who you are.

In truth, all these identities emerge from ego, (the thought "I") and are transformed into your identification with your body, your emotions, and your thoughts; this identity you believe to be unique and separate from others. It is a very deep belief, primarily because your physical senses of sight, sound, touch, taste, and smell continually confirm that this is who you are. But is it? If we strip away your identity, your life story, your clothes, your body, what is left? What remains? What has been constant throughout your entire life? Who lives beyond physical life? Who is present when you are free? Who is present when you are not free?

It is That which is always constant, always present, always alive, always aware at the core of your being. That is the focus of this book. It is the essence of freedom; it is the eternal light of the eternal Self; it is pure conscious awareness, the infinite energy of all that is and ever was. It is That. You are That. It is the foundation of Truth that transcends all knowledge. Recognizing it for yourself is the ultimate gateway of freedom. That which eludes your senses is the Truth of who you are. All the great spiritual masters point to this great Truth: You are the divine light of the infinite pure conscious awareness, known as God, the Self, Atman, the Cosmos. You are That! You are nothing more and nothing less.

To fully comprehend this, you must stop and recognize the story of you, created by you and maintained by you. It is this very deep belief in your story that begins with the I-thought, or ego, that causes you to believe, think, and act as a separate, unique person. The challenge here is to recognize that while you are a unique person with a unique body and your own personal story, freedom asks that you allow yourself for just a moment to recognize something hidden, something so close to you that it is closer than your breath, something you already know deep in the very core of your bones.

Freedom invites you to stop and acknowledge a deep unknowable longing that has always been present for as long as you can remember. You might recognize it as a longing for peace, for enlightenment or for something that will end your own suffering. When you stop to examine this longing more closely, you will discover that it is something ancient, indestructible, peaceful, and silent. You might have attempted to satisfy this longing with people, places, and things only to find that ultimately nothing seems to satisfy this deep longing. When you realize this, there is a kind of disillusionment with life that can be experienced as a tiny crack or a huge gulf between what you thought your life was all about and the emptiness of recognizing on some level that it is not that. Whether it is perceived as a tiny crack or a huge gulf, this disillusionment with life is the spark that ignites the sacred flame of your eternal nature. This sacred fire leads you to the ocean of bliss that will quench your seemingly unquenchable thirst for freedom, this deep mysterious longing within the core of your being.

This fire enables you to begin to notice something deep within you. When the sacred fire begins to burn, you naturally stop, and in this stopping, you move beyond your identification with the body or ego. This stopping is necessary in order to move to a new awareness of what is known as the Self, an awareness of who you really are beyond the construct of your ego. It is not enough to understand these concepts intellectually. You must stop following your thoughts outward to the world of people, places, and things and instead turn your attention inward to the

of your eternal nature. Freedom is as simple as letting go. You might still be wondering, "How?" The answer lives when you simply stop following your thoughts outward and instead turn your attention to where your thoughts came from in the first place. It takes only a fraction of a second to notice the source of all thought when you stop touching, clinging to, or identifying with any thought.

If you want to be free, simply stop clinging to anything physical, mental, or emotional in this moment. Too scary? Perhaps. Too challenging? Maybe. Too easy? Yes, it is that easy; it is that simple. As Gangaji, a student of Papaji, once said, *"Truth is simple and cannot be practiced."* There is no *doing* in Truth. As easily as dropping a pen to the floor, you can free yourself from identities and concepts. Do not worry. You can always pick up your identities again if you choose to. Truth lives in recognizing that you have

identities, but that these identities are not who
you are. Who you really are lives beyond any
identity or concept; it is the realization that
you are That, the infinite unknowable Self, the
cosmos of pure conscious awareness.

Please take a moment to re-visit the
questions: *Who says you are free? Who says you are
not free?* Did you notice how many things
(money, for example) can answer both
questions? These are not casual questions.
They can lead you directly into the depth of
the infinite Self, but only if you are willing to
use the power of your awareness to stop and
inquire about this "who." It requires that you
look beyond the concept of *who says you are free*
to another view of the same question: *Who is
aware that you are free or not free? Who is the subject,
the seer? Find this seer!* Now, what did you
notice? Who is the who, beyond your name
and who you think you are? Who is asking the
question? Now you are getting somewhere

and you are getting nowhere; *this* is what is meant by stopping. It is the going nowhere or stopping, to become aware of That which has always been here, always been present in every moment of your life.

You are at the very beginning of a new understanding of the Self, through the gateway of your own ego or the idea that you are this person, this body. What lives beyond ego? Where did the thought "I" emerge from? Find the source of the thought "I" and you will recognize what Jesus meant when He said, *"The kingdom of God is within you."* Remember, ego is not a bad thing; it is not something that you need to get rid of or destroy. Ego creates the context for you to begin your search for freedom. The thought "I must be free" comes from ego.

Be careful: Ego is a double-edged sword. On one edge, it can be the gateway to freedom; on the other, it can be an endless barrier to freedom. Ego, as a gateway, opens your consciousness to the idea that freedom exists. However, ego by its very nature suggests that you are separate from everything and everyone; from the ego's perspective freedom is not here, so it must be somewhere else. This idea that freedom is somewhere else causes you to search for it, but this search is a delusion caused by your ego. The act of seeking transforms freedom into some type of object – perhaps a sacred object, but an object nonetheless.

As the gateway of your ego opens, you begin to search and you believe yourself to be the seeker, a person who is looking for something sacred, something secret. This seeker is separate from the object that is sought or that which is to be attained: true and lasting freedom or enlightenment. Seeker, object, path, and attainment are the ultimate tricks of the ego. You are actually being led down a path that does not exist, toward a sacred object that is nowhere, creating the context for never finding what you are seeking! Sounds like a bad dream, doesn't it?

Your continued search for freedom feeds right into the ego. You are conditioned to think that you must *do* something in order to receive something. Because you believe that you are your body, you naturally think that you are the "doer," which means that you must take action if you are going to free yourself. This belief that you are the *doer* started you on the path to enlightenment. It is the ego's desire, "I have to be free," which initially opens gateway of Truth. Or as Jesus points out, "For every one who asks receives, and he who seeks finds, and to him who knocks it will be opened." However, the ego's idea, "Freedom is not here, so it must be somewhere else," combined with the belief that you are the *doer*, causes the search for freedom to continue and the gateway closes. Do you see how tricky ego can be? The very thing that opens the gateway of Truth almost instantly transforms into a barrier that can keep you from ever finding what you are searching for.

The Truth is, you already have what you are looking for. You have always been the infinite peace, happiness, and freedom that enlightenment promises. You are freedom itself. But until you discover this for yourself, it does not matter who tells you it is true; it does not matter how many spiritual teachers you meet, or how many austerities you perform, or how many spiritual books you read. None of these will provide you the elusive freedom that you seek.

Even this book will ultimately be meaningless unless you stop for just a moment and turn your attention back to the source of the I-thought. When you turn your awareness to the source of the ego, the sense of being the *doer* will naturally fall away and you will be at peace, you will be happy, you will recognize your own enlightenment. You do not have to get rid of the *doer* or ego. These ideas of who you are will naturally vanish the second you turn your mind towards its source.

At this point you might begin to see how ego can lead you to seeking, but that seeking is not leading you where you ultimately want to go. Like a dog chasing its tail, you just spin and spin and spin, thinking you are getting somewhere, only to discover that you are going nowhere. At this point you can begin to recognize that nothing you *do* seems to produce the lasting result that you have been looking for.

If you were not seeking something – enlightenment, peace, or simply happiness –

you probably would not have picked this book up. Mysteriously, the Grace of the unknowable Self has already touched your heart, providing you an opportunity to step into a sacred fire, the eternal flame of your own freedom. This unknowable Grace is offering you the gift of eternal, permanent, indescribable happiness. It is an unknowable living presence that is alive in your own heart, in everyone's heart.

Be careful or you might find yourself *trying* to see the source of the I-thought. Remember, any attempt to "do" or "try" only acts to reinforce the idea that there is a *doer*. Trying is a needless effort that only creates a barrier to freedom. There is literally no doing required. When you stop everything for just a moment, a natural realization will occur. A great example of *non-doing* is when you fall asleep. There is no effort in sleeping; you just fall asleep. But what happens when you sleep?

The obvious answer is that your body has a chance to rest, but what happens to your consciousness, your awareness? Have you ever noticed that when you drift off to sleep you lose consciousness of your surroundings? When you are sleeping everything you know – your identity, your clothes, your room, your house, your lover, your husband, your wife, how you look, your problems – all fall away as you surrender into sleep.

Once you fall asleep you begin to dream. When you are dreaming, your body is sleeping while your awareness is focused on the story of the dream, which can seem just as real as anything that might happen to you when you are awake. Of course, you are always relieved when you realize the monster that was chasing you was just a dream and not real. Because of your natural perception and ability to discern, you know that dreams are not real, but they can seem very real when you are sleeping. When you wake up, your attention returns to the continuing story of you. It might be a good story or a bad story, but your awareness is focused outward onto the story. From this perspective, the waking and dream states are identical. In the dream state, your awareness is focused on the dream story; in the waking state, your awareness is focused on your life story. In both instances, the dream or life story seems real. The opportunity is for you to recognize that the things you experience when you are awake are constantly changing, just as the things you experience when you are dreaming. The tricky part is that your perception of the world is based on your physical experience (sight, hearing, taste, touch, and smell); on your emotional experience (how you feel about what you are perceiving); and on your mental experience (what you think about what you are experiencing). The physical, emotional, and mental aspects of your story work together to create the belief that your story is real. In this context, the world you experience is more real than the world of your dreams, because your physical senses reinforce the belief that the world you experience is real. But have you ever noticed that nothing you experience, no matter how physical, emotional, or mental, ever remains exactly the same, even if you attempt to re-enact the original experience? The truth is that nothing lasts in this world. Your body, emotions, and thoughts are always changing, moving, flowing. Your dreams, life, and even the world are always changing. In the end, anything that changes is not real. The challenge here is to become aware of that which does not change: the awareness that is present when you are awake and also present when your body sleeps. As the Bhagavad Gita so eloquently states: *"There is no existence*

of the unreal and no non-existence of the real."
Ultimately, the Self is the one infinite constant
consciousness that permeates everything –
That which does not change.

There is another state of consciousness
that exists when you are not awake and you
are not dreaming. This is the state in between
the waking and dream states known as the
sleep state. In this sleep state you are not aware
of anything in the physical world and you are
not dreaming, yet you are aware. In this state,
you experience your natural feelings of peace,
happiness, and freedom – *being-consciousness-
bliss*, known in India as *sat-chit-ananda*. When
you are in the waking or dream states you can
feel all kinds of emotions – happy, sad, glad,
fearful – and you can have all kinds of
experiences – good, bad, happy, or scary; yet,
in the in-between state called sleep you feel
only peace and happiness. Why is that? Why

do you experience peace and happiness in the sleep state?

When you are in the sleep state, the story of you has disappeared, yet you remain aware. You are not aware of your body, your story, your emotions, your beliefs, or even your surroundings. In fact, the you as you think yourself to be is completely non-existent, yet you are aware. When you wake up from the sleep state, you feel refreshed and you are aware that you were asleep, but while you were in the sleep state nothing existed except consciousness itself. When you sleep, you are naturally letting go of your story and are surrendering into the bliss of the unknowable Self. The challenge is to remain in the sleep state while you are awake! This means to let go of your story and remain aware of awareness itself.

You might not have even been aware that there is state of consciousness that lives between waking and dreaming. You might not be aware of the sleep state at all. You might not even notice that who you think you are has completely vanished. Like most people, you might only know that you relish a good night's sleep – but have you ever stopped to contemplate why this is true?

You have an opportunity here to stop and recognize that during sleep you have no past, present, or future; you simply exist in the moment as *being-consciousness-bliss*. You have an opportunity to experience the sleep state while you are awake, which enables you to recognize what has always been free from your ego or simply the story of you. When you sleep while you are awake, it is possible to experience simply *being* and recognize the complete and total union with Self or God that is present in every moment, whether or not you are consciously aware of it. When you are free from your association with the body, mind, thoughts, emotions, sounds, and images, all that is left is your eternal Self.

The only feeling associated with the Self is pure silent love, which is your natural state of being. The recognition of the Self is not possible as long as your awareness is focused outward toward the story created in either the waking or dream states. Take a moment right here, right now and completely let go of the story of you and deeply contemplate the question: *Who sleeps?* Allow yourself to notice That which is aware even in the sleep state. That which lives beyond the gateway of the ego is what you want to focus your entire awareness on.

You are at a critical point of recognizing your own enlightenment. To be enlightened is to recognize that your conditioned existence, that is, all the things that you have used throughout your life to define who you are (body, mind, past, identity,

25

conditioning), are really just aspects of the story of you and are not really who you are. Freedom requires that you let it all go, especially the story of you that has been created and maintained by you.

At its core, ego is the I-thought, the source of all discordant thoughts and feelings. Ego can be a gateway or a barrier to freedom. The ego as a gateway leads directly to your eternal freedom when you turn your entire awareness to the source of the primal I-thought. The choice of ego as a barrier or gateway is completely and totally yours and yours alone to make.

Now we will take a deeper look into the meaning of Mind. What is Mind? Where is it?

Mind

Like ego, what is known as *Mind* emerges from the primal I-thought. It can be thought of as a lens that is focused either outward to the world or inward toward the source of all thought. For most people the mind is focused outward, reinforcing the sense that there is *somebody* looking out toward the world. When the mind is focused inward toward the source of itself, then this somebody naturally cannot be found and the mind itself disappears.

Mind is past. It is the story that comes into existence with the primal I-thought, or ego, and gains strength through your experiences. You cannot have a story without first having the thought "I" and you can't have a story without a past, right? Mind comprises both subconscious and conscious stories, which operate through the physical, emotional, and mental aspects of your ego. It is a continuum of sensations and feelings and thoughts. As long as the lens of your mind is focused outward toward the world of people, places, and things, this mind continuum continues to flow, creating the constantly evolving story of you as a separate and unique person.

All thought emerges from pure consciousness or Self, which moves through the lens of your mind into and through your physical form. As thoughts move into mind, you experience them as I-sensations, I-thoughts, and I-feelings. Mind emerges from the infinite Self, not from the brain of the body. There is an endless stream of thoughts that flow out of and into the Self through what is known as mind, which is not limited to your physical form. How do you know this to be true? Take a moment to notice your thoughts. *Where do these thoughts emerge from and disappear into?*

Buddha's heart sutra explains, *"Form is Emptiness and Emptiness is Form."* All thought emerges from and returns to the vast emptiness of the Self. It is through the emptiness of the Self that we perceive form, and at the very core of any form is emptiness. Mind itself is emptiness and cannot exist without the Self. It is not an object that you can point to. It serves as a lens or gateway between the Self and the physical form, enabling you to become aware of your surrounding environment as well as the thoughts that emerge from the Self and return to the Self. Ultimately, mind and thoughts are completely empty. They come from nothing and contain nothing. To discover this for yourself, simply penetrate any one of your thoughts with your awareness and you will discover that at the core of any thought is pure, silent emptiness.

The average person has thousands of thoughts in a single day. This incessant movement of thoughts through your mind can be a source of frustration, becoming the catalyst for seeking peace or a method for stopping the mind. Many spiritual communities use meditation as a method for stopping the mind. Meditation is commonly believed to be one of the most effective practices for stopping the incessant chatter of the mind and is often believed to be the method required for attaining the state of enlightenment. This belief alone can render meditation completely ineffective.

When you approach meditation from the perspective of a method to get something, even if it is simply out of the desire to stop the incessant chatter of your mind, the ego (I-thought) has taken over. The belief is: "If *I* meditate, *I* will stop my mind, and if *I* stop my mind, *I* will attain the state of enlightenment (i.e., *I* will be peaceful)." Do you see the fallacy in this? From the perspective of "What will *I* get," meditation is transformed into a strategy for *doing* something in order to get something. It requires effort and it requires a *doer*.

True meditation requires no effort and can occur any time, anywhere – on a busy street corner or in a quiet temple hidden deep in the Himalayan Mountains. Meditation is effortless, silent, and peaceful. When meditation becomes a strategy, it transforms into a kind of concentration that can be both physically and mentally painful, as the endless stream of thoughts continues to plague you. This is the primary reason that most people do not enjoy meditation – especially the first few times they attempt it.

Meditation as a method creates a trap, reinforcing the idea that you are the *doer*, that if you *do* meditation, you will force the mind to stop. Once you are free from your monkey mind, you will have finally found the Holy Grail – the golden fruit of enlightenment. Do you see how *doing* meditation is simply a continuation of the story of you? Can you see how ego as a barrier to freedom has slipped in here? When meditation becomes a strategy for attaining enlightenment, whether you are aware of it or not, you are telling yourself that enlightenment is somewhere else and you must meditate or *do* something in order to get it. Meditation from this perspective will be ineffective, simply because *you* cannot stop your mind. Trying to stop your mind is like trying to stop the sun from rising; it is not possible as long as you think you are the *doer*. This does not mean that meditation does not have value, but meditation as a method will not stop the incessant activity of the mind. Freedom simply asks that you turn your attention to the source of the *doer* or the source of the mind itself. The mind will naturally stop its incessant chatter the moment your awareness is turned toward its source. Once you see the source of the mind the mind itself will vanish. When there is no mind meditation will arise of its own accord.

Of course, as you move through your life you must look outward to the world of people, places, and things. This is the nature of everyone's life. In order to live, you must engage with your surroundings. Even if you retreat to some remote meditation cave you still must look outward through the lens of your mind to interact with your surroundings. This looking outward is necessary for the survival of your physical body. After all, your body needs food, clothing, and shelter in order for it to survive, doesn't it? Mind is also the catalyst for sex or procreation of the physical form to ensure that the species survives. The primal desire of survival and procreation is the initial force that causes the mind to turn toward the objects desired instead of inward toward the infinite peace of the Self.

The desire to survive and continue the species is one aspect of mind. Another aspect of mind is thought. Thought is a form of energy, the spark of creation that moves through the lens of your mind. It is through your thoughts that you create, that you manifest your experience of life. Any thought you focus on long enough must manifest in your experience as an action, emotion, or creation. Everything you see – in fact, the world itself – came into existence as a direct result of thought.

The Bible says, *"In the beginning was the Word and the Word was with God and the Word was God."* What came before the Word? What is present before any thought? When you contemplate this deeply you will discover the most profound, empty silence that precedes any thought and is contained within every thought! Every word contains this silent pure presence of the Self, of God; there is no separation. It is through the silent emptiness of the Cosmos, God, or Self that all things emerge from and return to. To recognize this for yourself, notice the space among the thoughts that emerge from consciousness. This empty space is a reservoir of pure conscious love, the source of all thought which lives in the most sacred of all places, your own heart. This is why Buddha called his recognition that *"Form is Emptiness and Emptiness is Form"* the Heart Sutra! All form emerges from and returns to the Self through the heart. The heart is the gateway to God. Did you ever wonder why there are so many pictures of Jesus pointing to his heart? He was literally pointing to the gateway of eternal freedom, which lives in your own heart.

Freedom does not live in your head or brain. You cannot think your way to enlightenment. It is not your mind that enables you to perceive the infinite nature of the Self. It is the sacred gateway of the heart, at the very core of your being, that enables you to perceive the Self. When you turn your mind toward its source, your mind will naturally fall into your sacred heart (the very core of your being). Again, there really is no doing on your part!

From this perspective you can begin to understand what Jesus meant when he said, *"Know the Truth and the Truth will make you free."* Did you notice that there is no *doing* and there is no *doer* in that statement? In this single statement, He is pointing to the Truth that once you recognize ("know") the Truth the

Truth itself will *make* you free; the mind in this case is a gateway to freedom. Like the ego, the mind can either be a gateway into the vast unknowable reservoir of consciousness or a barrier that blocks you from recognizing this infinite reservoir of *being-consciousness-bliss.* The choice is yours and yours alone.

To recognize this for yourself, you have to stop for just a moment, be still, and be quiet. Once you are still, your mind will naturally turn toward the source of all thought. There is never a moment void of the eternally free, silent presence within you. Your enlightened pure awareness is always present, never absent. However, if you are focused on the thoughts, feelings, and images that emerge in your mind, you will not notice this silent presence. You will be completely distracted by your incessant conversation within your own mind.

Ramana often used watching a movie as a metaphor to help people understand the dynamics of the mind. When you go to the movies, you see images flashed upon a stationary screen. The movie itself is a strip of celluloid film with a series of still images printed on it. When the film moves through the projector, the light inside the projector projects these images onto the movie screen. As the still images move through the projector they are flashed onto the screen in rapid succession, creating the illusion that the images are moving. As the story begins to unfold, you sit watching the movie, absorbed in the story portrayed by these images; you are seeing the movie, the drama. When you are watching the movie, there are things that you are not seeing: the light that projects the images, the lens that focuses the images, and the screen upon which the images are projected.

Using the movie as a metaphor, the light of the projector (Self) is filtered through your thoughts (film), focused outward through your mind (lens), and projected through the senses of the body (projector), which all work together to create the illusionary images of the world (movie) projected onto the Self (screen). When you are absorbed in the constantly changing images of your thoughts (film), which are projected through your own mind (lens) you are mesmerized by the story they create (movie). While your awareness is focused on your story (movie) you do not see the source of the movie, which is the light (Self). When the lens (mind) is inverted toward the light, your awareness is focused on the source of the story (movie), which is the light of the projector (Self). Once you see the light (Self), there is no film (thoughts); there is no lens (mind); there is no projector (body); and there is no story (movie) to watch. All that is seen is the *seer*, the constant light of the Self.

Did you notice that the Self is the *light* and the *screen* upon which the light is projected? This can be confusing to the mind. You might be thinking, "How can the Self be both?" The Self is omniscient; it is the Alpha and the Omega – the beginning (light) and the end (screen); the eternal constant. If there are no thoughts (film) or movie (story) to watch, what would you see? Whether you are looking at the screen or the light of the projector, all that is seen is the light of the Self!

The Self is so much a part of who you already are, so close it is before your breath, that it eludes your ordinary way of thinking. In the context of the eternal unknowable Self, nothing that appears real is real, and everything that is real cannot be seen with your physical eyes. What is important is literally invisible to the eyes. To recognize what is real, you must begin to perceive what is beyond the physical world that you can see, hear, taste, touch, and smell. You must begin to notice what is always present, always constant, within your own heart. You must stop, be still, and be quiet in order to move beyond the limitations of your mind, to experience no-mind. When you stop following your thoughts, feelings, and images that live in your mind and instead turn your attention toward the source of all thought, the Truth will reveal itself to you. Once again, there is absolutely no *doing*.

A shift in your awareness is required, from one of thinking to *being*. By simply *being*, you naturally become aware of the Truth. *Being* means to stop for a moment so that you can become aware of what is already here, rather than trying to move to get something that you *think* is somewhere else. There is absolutely no doing required to recognize That which is present within you. The only requirement is that you stop and pay attention to That which is always present.

We have just explored two of the most powerful gateways of consciousness – ego and mind – which, for most of us, are barriers to freedom. Let's take a closer look at another gateway of freedom: Time. How can time free you or keep you in bondage?

Time

Time is a concept that emerges from ego and mind. Like ego and mind, time also emerges from the primal I-thought as a record of your experiences. Time is a linear arrangement of I-experiences, I-images, and I-thoughts. It works in conjunction with the ego and the mind to maintain the story of you. Time enables you to distinguish among past, present, and future. In spiritual communities, it is a very common belief that the goal of spiritual practice is to get rid of your ego, stop the mind, and stay in the moment. Time, from this perspective, is transformed into the belief that if you remain aware in the moment you will access the power of "now" and free yourself from your past. This belief hides the truth that any attempt you make to stay in the moment immediately separates you from the moment.

The moment is always here right now, whether or not you are aware of it. You are the moment itself, the Cosmos. Trying to stay in the moment is an attempt to hold onto the experience of the moment or access the power of it. Any attempt to maintain or hold onto anything is another trap of the ego.

When you attempt to "stay in the moment," the moment itself becomes a thought, which objectifies time into yet another thing to get or to hold onto, which only lives in the realm of ego or primal I-thought. Time as a trap emerges with the idea, "*I* must try to stay in the moment to free myself from my past and access the power of *now*." In truth, there is no *trying* to be in the moment. How can you avoid the moment? You can totally space out or daydream and still be in the moment! Trying to be in the moment ultimately causes you to attempt to hold onto your concept of the present instead of recognizing that you *are* the moment, free from the past or future or even the present moment. When you recognize that you are the moment, then you are free to simply "be."

Your life is fluid like a flowing river. When you *try* to hold onto this moment, it is like trying to hold onto the water that is flowing through the river; it is impossible. Any concept you have of this moment lives in the mind, which is already past. Even the thought "*I* must remain in the present" is already in the past.

Freedom lives in the recognition of That which is timeless in time, that which has no beginning, middle, or end. It lives in the recognition that there is no time at all – past, present, or future. At first, this might be difficult to grasp, since we all live our lives based on time. There is a birth (beginning), a middle (life), and an end (death). Anything that is born must also die. But what is it that never dies?

You use time every day of your life, as a practical measurement that enables you to meet with a friend, to determine when something should be taken out of the oven, or to determine the winner of a race. From this perspective, time is an effective tool that you use every day without much consideration. It is not something you can get rid of or hold onto in order to gain your freedom.

Time is a constant measurement that is in constant motion, like sand through an hourglass, constant yet moving. Depending on what is going on in your life, you can experience time as flying by or seeming to stand still. When you are waiting in line at a movie theater, fifteen minutes can seem like an eternity; but when you are enjoying a boat ride in the ocean, fifteen minutes passes by in what seems to be just a few seconds. The first time that you meditate, fifteen minutes can seem to stretch into hours. Time is always constant, but your experience of time changes in relationship to what is happening around you and works to maintain the story of you. When you recognize that time is in constant motion, it becomes much easier to recognize that time, like your life, is fluid and cannot be held onto.

Time flows through the moment as a record of your experiences. Any experience you have is finished the very instant it is experienced. All of your life experiences (I-experiences) live only in your memory, as a loose collection of I-images, I-feelings, and I-thoughts. They create the story of you, which lives only in your mind, which is past. Pure awareness has no concept of time. This is why a past memory can seem as real to you in this moment as it was when it was actually occurring. When your awareness is placed on these memories – the collections of images, thoughts, and feelings – you immediately experience the past in the moment. This can cause a tremendous amount of suffering. The moment you identify with past thoughts, you have placed, either consciously or unconsciously, your awareness away from its source onto your story, reinforcing the egoic belief that you are separate from God. This belief is the root cause of all forms of suffering. A word of caution here: *New Age* thinking equates union with God with the idea, *"I am God."* This idea can deify the ego. As Arthur Osborne, a well-known author of Ramana's teachings, observed union with God is more accurately recognized as, *"I am not-other-than- God."* Arthur explained, *"When the illusionary other-than-God is denied, what remains? – Only God."*

Ultimately, freedom lives in the recognition of That which is free from ego, mind, and time. It lives in the recognition that even the "now" moment is a concept. When you fully recognize that time is a concept that lives only in your mind, you are free to see That which your concept of time emerged from: the timeless reservoir of pure consciousness that is always here within you and all around you. Who you really are is timeless in time. You are the timeless, ageless, pure, all-knowing Self. Freedom lives in recognizing this Truth for yourself.

Have you ever noticed that one minute you can be crying your eyes out and the next, laughing hysterically? Why is this so? Your awareness moves fast, like a flash of lightning. It moves so fast, you are not necessarily even aware of the images, thoughts, and feelings that you are identified with in any given moment. All you know is that you are experiencing anger, sadness, fear, or happiness. Since your awareness moves so quickly, you are very sure that you feel the way you do because of the circumstance you find yourself in, or you *think* it was caused by something someone else did or said to you. In truth, anything you are experiencing is a direct result of where you have placed your awareness. That's it; period; end of story.

When you focus your awareness on the images, words, and feelings you are having in any given moment, it is no different from watching a movie. When you are watching a movie, you are not seeing, feeling, or hearing anything other than the movie. Similarly, when you focus your awareness on the story that is in your mind, you are caught in a trance created by your own images, feelings, and thoughts. When you are in a trance you are not aware of anything else; you are at the effect of the images, feelings, and thoughts you are having. When you feel your sadness suddenly shift to happiness, it is simply because you shifted your awareness from one set of images, feelings, and thoughts to another. Your awareness is completely independent of time and can move so fast that you are not even aware of what is happening.

To discover this for yourself, take a moment right now and recall a recent experience in which someone said or did something that upset you. Now, stop completely for a moment; then gradually start to recall the experience. As you begin to remember the experience, slow your memory down and allow yourself to notice what actually happened. First, examine what happened: Write down on a piece of paper what the person did or said. Limit it to just what the person actually did or said, not including what you thought or felt. Please keep this to a simple two- or three-sentence summary. Now take a moment to examine what thoughts or images you had in mind and what you felt when the person did or said something; write that down. Now, write down what you heard, thought, felt, and saw in that moment. Notice what you imagined that it meant about you and what you thought that it meant about them. Did you notice how you start to feel upset again right now in this moment by focusing on these same sounds, images, thoughts and feelings that you wrote down?

Focusing on thoughts associated with a past experience represents the natural tendency of mind to explain *why* things happened which leads you into a story about what happened. When you focus on this story you will experience the same thoughts, feelings and images associated with the story. When you slow down your memory, it gives you an opportunity to investigate *how* you experienced this situation. This inquiry into *how* you experienced it has nothing to do with right and wrong, it simply represents an opportunity to see how you experienced this situation that ultimately led you to feeling upset.

When you look at what you wrote down about this particular incident, instead of focusing on the circumstances of what happened, focus instead on what happened within you. How did your reaction to this experience manifest? Did you *feel* something first, or did you *think* something first? Was it the sound of the other person's voice that triggered this feeling, or was it a thought about what she or he said? This is like playing a movie backwards; you want to trace your reaction back to *how* it began. When you look to see the thoughts, images, and feelings associated with this past experience, you can begin to recognize that what happened within you created the feeling of being upset – not what the person did or said! This is worth repeating. It is what happened within you that created the feeling of being upset – not what the person did or said! Do you see *how* this works? It is what you place your awareness on that creates your experience.

Let's take this a step further – turn the paper over and simply stop. Stop. Did I mention stop? What occurs when you no longer identify with your I-images, I-thoughts, and I-feelings associated with this experience? When you drop all of it, what happens? What do you experience? If you are successful in detaching from any thought, word, or feeling you have in this moment, you will experience the pure happiness of the Self. If you are not experiencing that, then check to see what images, thoughts, and feelings you are identifying with. It is really simple. If you want to be free, you need to recognize the words, thoughts, and feelings that you are following outward and *stop following them.* It does not matter who was right or wrong; this is another trick of mind. It is mind attempting to justify the thoughts, feelings, and words. Freedom lives in releasing all words, thoughts, and feelings to see what is deeper, to see the *seer.*

The substratum of all existence is where your ultimate freedom resides. That which is common to all events in history is common to all events and experiences of your own life as well. Every moment of your life – the good, the bad, and the downright ugly – emerge from the infinite substratum of pure consciousness. It is this substratum that you want to turn your mind toward, That which lives beyond time. Once you turn your mind toward its source, your ego, mind and time naturally fall away, enabling you to fully recognize the source of all thought. When you focus on the source, *or follow your thoughts, feelings, and images inward*, you will discover the ultimate freedom for yourself. Another way of looking at this is the substratum as the light of the projector and the events of your life as the film. The one thing that all the events in your life have in common is the light of the projector, the constant infinite light of the Self.

Let's try a simple exercise to help you recognize this for yourself. I invite you to make a list of all your identities on a plain sheet of paper. Please keep it to one sheet of paper, or this exercise might take you weeks to complete. On a second sheet of paper, write down the highlights of your life: where you were born, where you grew up, where you live now, and a short summary of your life experiences. Now you have two sheets of paper, one filled with all your identities and another filled with a summary of your life experiences. Now contemplate the following questions for a moment: *What is common to all of my various identities? What is common to all my life experiences? What is common to all my identities and all my life experiences combined?*

Notice what is revealed through contemplating these questions. Using the paper to illustrate this further, we can see that what is common to all your identities is the paper they are written on. The same would be true for your life experiences; throughout all identities and all experiences, the paper is common to both. Now let's use the paper as a metaphor of the divine Truth of who you are. The paper now represents the reservoir of pure conscious love, the infinite Self, the constant Source of all that is. From this perspective you can begin to see that all your identities and experiences have this one thing in common: They all emerge from and return to this great Self, the Pure Consciousness of all that is. Beyond all time, experience, and identity is the constant, unimaginable reservoir of consciousness that gives you life itself.

Let's take a moment to look at the story of your life. Notice that when you remember your past, it appears very real. But in this moment right here, right now ask yourself: Is it real? Is it happening right now in this moment? Are the people, places, and things you describe in your past around you now exactly as they were then? Can you show this past to anyone, or can you only explain it? Is it real or is it memory?

Your past is real only in your memory. The experiences you had when you were eight years old are over; they are no longer happening. Have you ever thought that things could have been different if you had only done this and not done that? Or that your life would be perfect if you had only taken that job, or if you had only asked that girl out the first time you saw her?

This is how the mind works. It creates a story based on experiences, which are made up of images, thoughts, and feelings. In your mind you analyze the story to see if it could possibly be made into a better story, or you make decisions regarding what it means about you or someone else. The funny thing here is that in your mind you are not satisfied with the past the way it was. You have the idea, "I should have done this or that differently, and then my life would be so much better!" This is truly amazing. You are attempting to go back to the past, which no longer exists, in an effort to change it. If you could change the decisions you made in the past, then the story of your life would be so much better here in the present. Now you have entered into the process of trying to change what was not even really here in the first place!

By letting go of your concept of time and simply not identifying with your story, you will recognize that you are the moment – you are the Cosmos. When you recognize that you are the moment, you will know that who you are is permanent, indescribable happiness, the infinite love of the Self. When time transforms into this recognition that you are the moment – always free from the past, present, or future – then the moment itself becomes a gateway to freedom. Time, from this perspective, is a gateway to the infinite. When you identify with your story, your history, then time becomes a shackle that will keep you tied to the ever-evolving story of you, directed by ego, produced by mind, with you as the leading actor. Letting go of your concept of time as past-present-future enables you to relax and accept your life right now, just as it is. When you stop judging or trying to change what happened in the past and simply allow yourself to accept what is right here, right now in this moment, (independent from thoughts, feelings, and images) you will experience a natural feeling of expansion. This is the freedom of simply *Being*.

Now you have an opportunity to look at your past from a new perspective: It is a story, maybe a very interesting story, but still just a story. It does not define who you really are unless you allow it to. If you want to be free from your story, it is as simple as crumpling up the paper and throwing it out! It is gone, finished, over and done with; it is not real. Let it go. Stop identifying with it. For just one moment, let it go. Stop trying to keep it, fix it, change it, or modify it. I really mean this. If you want to be free, you have to stop identifying with your story, with all those I-experiences, I-thoughts, I-feelings, and I-images that are paths to the past. If you can let all this go, and recognize that you are the moment, you have taken the first step toward the ultimate freedom. You have started to stop.

Ego, mind, and time are all either gateways or barriers to freedom. Ultimately, the choice is yours. Now, let's take a moment to understand why attachment and desire work to either free you or keep you locked in the bondage of suffering. What causes you to continue to suffer?

Desire & Attachment

After his enlightenment, Buddha's first teaching consisted of what he called the *four noble truths*. The first noble truth is the recognition that there is suffering; that birth, decay, death, sorrow, pain, grief, and despair are all suffering. The second is that the root of all suffering is desire. The third is that once you are detached from desire, there is a complete extinction of the hatred, greed, and delusion caused by desire. This extinction is called *nirvana* or enlightenment, *the unshakeable deliverance of the Heart*. The forth is that there is a path that leads to the cessation of all suffering. This is called the middle path.

In this teaching Buddha reveals that desire is the root of all suffering and that detachment from it *is* nirvana or enlightenment. In many spiritual communities, this recognition has evolved into the belief that you must *do* something to become detached from desire. It is based in the idea that desire, like the ego, leads to suffering, so it is something to get rid of or suppress. It stems from the core belief that enlightenment requires the renunciation of the object world or the idea that, "Through the suppression of desire, I will attain enlightenment, which will give me special powers." Ultimately, there is no difference between spiritual desire (suppression of desires) and worldly desire (the acting out of desires).

Like mind and ego, desire stems from the primal I-thought. The idea "I want" or "I need" is the root of desire. It stems from the primal desire for the survival of the body. The desire for food, protection, shelter, and sex works to ensure that the physical body survives and that the propagation of the species continues. Desire is the primal I-force that propels the body and mind outward. At its core, desire is the idea that you must *do* something in order to get something. Whether it is a worldly or a spiritual desire, your attention is on what you have *versus* what you do not have, which causes you to continue to pursue the fulfillment of your desires. It works in conjunction with ego, mind, and time to ensure that the story of you continues.

This can seem a little confusing, since you might have had the experience that when you have pursued your desire, for example, the desire to get a new car, you feel happy when you have obtained the new car. The happiness that emerges once you have obtained the car can leave you with the idea that it was *the car* or *getting* the car that produced the feeling of happiness. The feeling of happiness produced by getting the desired object fools your mind into thinking that getting what you want produces the feeling of happiness. This leads to more and more desire.

This idea "I will be happy when I get what I want" is the fuel for pursuing more relationships, money, and things from a worldly perspective. It is also the fuel for renouncing desire from a spiritual perspective or the belief that "I will get enlightened if I suppress my desires." In truth, it is not acting out or suppressing desire that produces the feeling of happiness. The feeling of happiness naturally occurs the moment that you are empty of desire. In other words, you experience your natural state the moment you no longer have desire.

Desire ultimately leads to suffering either because you did not get what you thought you wanted or even though you got what you wanted, you still thirst for more. This thirst for more emerges naturally when you have the desire to maintain the happiness you experienced once you were *empty* of desire. You might eventually realize that once you have everything you thought you wanted, you are still not happy. You begin to realize that all the things you thought would make you happy do not produce the lasting happiness that you were seeking. From a spiritual perspective, you might recognize that suppression of desire does not produce the peace that enlightenment promises. It seems that there is always a desire for *something else* that will satisfy this seemingly unquenchable thirst for happiness. Ultimately, either acting out or suppressing desire leads to many forms of suffering.

The truth is, whether you act out or suppress your desire, desire will lead only to continued physical, mental, and emotional suffering. As Gangaji once said, *"If you practice desire, you will suffer."* To free yourself from the suffering caused by desire requires that you stop in the middle, between the two extremes of action and suppression. Buddha called this the *middle path*, which he described as the Noble Eightfold Path that leads to the extinction of suffering, namely: *Right Understanding, Right Thought, Right Speech, Right Action, Right Livelihood, Right Effort, Right Mindfulness,* and *Right Concentration.* This simply means that once you stop in the *middle* and *witness* desire, while remaining still and not acting out or suppressing desire, the Noble Eightfold Path will naturally occur. In other words, stopping is the *middle path* of enlightenment and the Noble Eightfold Path is the result of enlightenment – not the method for attaining it. As Buddha explained, *"Just as the rock of one solid mass remains unshaken by the wind, even so neither forms, nor sounds, nor odors, nor tastes, nor contacts of any kind, neither the desired or the undesired, can cause such a one to waver.*" When you *stop* in the *middle*, not acting out or suppressing your desire, then there is a natural burning of the desire that occurs. This is known as a *sacred fire*. Once desire transforms into a sacred fire, desire itself will naturally reveal its emptiness to you. When you meet your desires by not acting on them and not suppressing them – simply allowing yourself to burn in them – you see through the desire to the pure conscious silence that is eternally free from desire.

For most people, desire is a huge barrier to freedom and the catalyst for many forms of suffering. Desire transforms into a sacred gateway of enlightenment when the desire for freedom emerges into your consciousness. This desire for freedom is the only desire that consummates all other desires. It is a huge fire, where all other desires are consumed. In the end this fire will consume even your desire for freedom.

When you burn in this sacred fire, desire itself transforms into a gateway to freedom. Desire as a gateway returns you to your natural state, which is being-consciousness-bliss, the permanent happiness you are seeking. Desire as a barrier is a poison that undermines the recognition that you are freedom itself.

 Desire and attachment go hand and hand. Desire is the *doing to get*, while attachment is the *holding onto to keep*. Like desire, attachment emerges from the I-thought. The idea "I have" or "I will hold onto this or that" is the root of attachment. Like desire, attachment stems from the primal desire for the survival of the body. It reinforces the story of you: the idea that if you can just hold onto this experience, this person, or this thing in your life, then you life will be better and have more meaning.

 The more you attempt to hold onto something, the greater the burden of attachment. In many spiritual communities, it is very common for people to give away everything they own in an attempt to realize the freedom of non-attachment. Giving away everything you own does release the burden of attachment, producing the euphoric feeling of freedom. Once you have experienced the freedom produced by non-attachment, a subtle, maybe even unconscious, desire to hold onto the experience of freedom causes attachment to re-emerge. When the attachment re-emerges as the more subtle attachment to the experience of freedom, you will eventually return to the attachment of the object world of people, places, things, and experiences.

At its core, attachment is the idea, "Now that I have something, I am going to keep it," which reinforces the idea, "I am the doer" or "I am the owner." It works to ensure that your body and your story continue to exist. Attachment can be a barrier or a gateway to freedom. When you act on the impulse to attach or hold onto something or someone or an experience that you have had, your attention is outward on the object world and attachment becomes a barrier to freedom.

Once you recognize that even when you practice non-attachment, attachment can return. It is an opportunity to see that freedom is not about the stuff that you keep or give away; freedom lives in the recognition of something much deeper. It is a call to understand that the body and the three aspects of mind (I-feelings, I-thoughts, and I-sensations) are intertwined. They are irrevocably connected. There is a natural biological attachment between the body and mind, creating the continuum of the body-mind experience, which is rooted in survival. Nothing that you *do* to give away or keep has any impact on freedom. Freedom is always free from desire and attachment, which is a natural phenomenon of the body-mind continuum. As Papaji once said, *"The body is a desire body."*

When you stop "trying" to keep or give away, you have an opportunity to see through the body-mind attachment and recognize that there is a *seeingness*, a pure seeingness, that is already unattached to all of it. This seeingness has no problem with the body acting out its desires and attachments. When you stop following the desire to get or hold onto, you have an opportunity to become aware of this pure seeingness. You can recognize the Self within you, which is free from all of it. Attachment, like desire, becomes a poison when your life force, your awareness, is focused on getting, keeping, or giving away. Attachment becomes a gateway to freedom when you *stop* and focus your awareness through the body-mind, to see That

Release attachment & step into freedom (Heron's) workshop

which is alive in the very core of your being. It is at this core that you will discover a peace that surpasses all understanding. You will discover for yourself that freedom lives within you.

Freedom has nothing to do with attachment or non-attachment, desire or no desire. The pure awareness that holds it all is simply overlooked when your attention is focused on attachment or non-attachment, on acting out desire or suppressing desire. As Ramana once said, *"If you see the ring you do not see the gold."* Most people suffer because of their incessant pre-occupation with their own story and their attachment to their body and mind. Stated simply, suffering is a direct result of the images, thoughts, and feelings you are attached to in any given moment. As Gangaji once said, *"Suffering is complex and must be practiced to continue."* Just stop and think for a moment how much effort suffering requires.

It requires that you place your awareness on an image, thought, or feeling, and then think about what that means about you or someone else or what you need to do, get, or keep. As you continue to identify with thoughts, images, and feelings, you begin to believe they are real and you convince yourself that not only are they real, they are absolutely true, justified, even necessary. Most people are not even aware of the thoughts, images, and feelings that keep them trapped in endless cycles of suffering. In truth, freedom is always present regardless of the circumstances in your life: money or no money, relationship or no relationship, free or in prison, aware or not aware, happy or sad. True freedom is free from identification with anything. It is limitless, pure, conscious awareness. When you stop, your awareness has an opportunity to penetrate your natural biological attachment to the body-mind allowing this pure conscious awareness to reveal itself.

Have you ever wondered why Buddha became enlightened? The reason is very simple: He had the single desire to attain the state of nirvana or freedom, and when all else failed he *stopped* and sat under a Bodhi tree! He sat unmoving for days and he saw That which is unseen, That which is overlooked. As Buddha describes it, *"I discovered that profound truth, so difficult to perceive, difficult to understand, tranquillizing, and sublime, which is not to be gained by mere reasoning and is visible only to the wise."* Just like the Buddha, if you have the desire for freedom, the gateway of consciousness begins to open by itself, awakening the ancient fire of the infinite alive Truth within you the moment you stop following your desires.

The natural tendency of your mind is to follow your desires (I-thoughts, I-images, I-feelings, and I-sensations) outward toward the world. The challenge is to stop following them outward and instead look to see where they emerge. This is the gateway of enlightenment, the ultimate recognition of true freedom. It does not take years of spiritual practice to recognize this for yourself. Recognition happens faster than a finger snap. In truth, you are already enlightened. You are freedom itself. Enlightenment is not a thing or experience that you have to attain. Enlightenment is already here!

Freedom lives in the simple recognition that your natural body-mind, desires, and attachments have nothing to do with freedom. The more you burn in the fire of your own desires and attachments, by not acting on them or suppressing them, the hotter the fire becomes, naturally burning away all desire, all attachment. If, like the Buddha, you desire freedom above all else, the sacred fire will burn even the desire to be free; the sacred spark that ignited the flame of your eternal freedom and opened the gateway of consciousness. Allowing yourself to burn in this sacred fire will result in a clarity that will enable you to recognize That which has always been here, the conscious, alive presence within you that is free from desire and attachment, free from thoughts, feelings, and images. This sacred fire is like no other and will even burn away any idea you have about what freedom is. It begins with a simple invitation to *stop*, to let go and recognize the truth of who you are, beyond your story, beyond your desires, beyond even the most basic desire to survive.

The path to freedom is very narrow and very sharp. It is literally like walking on the edge of a razor, or as Buddha discovered, the middle path. Papaji illuminates, *"Don't carry a load on the razor's edge; even one thought is too much."* What would it be like to walk on a razor's edge? As Papaji suggests, even one thought is too much to carry. Freedom is like this; it is walking the razor's edge. It is standing in the middle between the two extremes of action and the suppression of desire and attachment. It is a stopping to recognize That which is and always has been free from any attachment and desire. It asks that you recognize the pure seeingness that is free from all of it, free from the endless stream of I-experiences, I-thoughts, I-feelings, and I-images that emerge from mind and body.

You have reached the point of no return. You have the opportunity in this moment, right now, to let go and burn in the sacred fire of desire. You have an opportunity to recognize That which lives beyond any attachment or desire. Please take a moment right here, right now, and stop acting out or suppressing any attachment or desire that you have. When you *stop* in this way, you give yourself the opportunity to see That which is untouched by either attachment or desire. Remember, desire and attachment can be either a gateway or a barrier to freedom. Even the most sacred spiritual practice of non-attachment becomes polluted by the subtle desire, "If I give everything away, I will gain my eternal freedom." If you want to be free, use your own awareness to pierce the bubble of your body-mind attachments, and soar on the wings of Grace.

Ego, mind, time, attachment, and desire – all of these can work together to open the gateway of your eternal freedom or to slam it shut. In the end, only you can decide between freedom or bondage. What is it that you believe? Are you free or not? How do your beliefs keep you in bondage, or how do they set you free forever?

Beliefs

All your beliefs are deeply rooted in the story of you. They emerge from the primal I-thought and evolve into complex concepts and ideas based on what you have read and experienced, or what you have been taught by your parents, society, and religion. Your beliefs are filtered through the body and the three primary aspects of mind (I-thoughts, I-feelings, and I-sensations). Over time, your beliefs might deepen into what you are certain is true. Beliefs are very powerful bundles of thoughts that develop into complex strategies for survival. These strategies can be conscious beliefs, or unconscious beliefs that have become second nature so you are not even aware that they exist.

Beliefs provide a structure for a way of being in relationship with others. For example, it is believed by society in general that the polite response is "thank you" when someone gives you something. "Thank you" is an automatic response for most people when they are given something as simple as a napkin at the dinner table. Beliefs also act as a form of measurement; they provide a structure for deciding between right and wrong, or what works and what does not. At their core, beliefs emerge from your own personal experience. If you were not taught by someone to say "thank you," it simply would not occur to you to say "thank you" when someone gives you something.

Because your beliefs are deeply rooted in the story of you, they can be either positive or negative, depending on what you have experienced and what you believe about yourself. Any thought you focus your awareness on long enough must manifest as a creation, emotion, or action. Your beliefs are very powerful bundles of thoughts, images, and feelings that are deeply rooted in your story. If you believe you are not good enough or not smart enough, you are actually manifesting the experience that you are *not good enough* and your outward life will reflect that. You might or might not be aware that you are living your life out of the belief that you are *not good enough* simply because this belief is deeply rooted in your life experience or your story. Over time, you have collected lots of evidence that what you believe to be true is actually true, based on your own experience. We often fail to recognize that any experience we are having is tied directly to what we believed in the first place! Belief creates the experience, which becomes part of the story, which ultimately creates a never-ending cycle that works to reinforce the original belief. For example, if someone did something terrible to you in the past, the experience of what that person did is over the moment it is over. What you believe about yourself, based on what this person did to you, is retained in your mind. You might believe that you are worthless or unlovable because of what this person did. After a period of time, this belief can become completely unconscious, and you have no idea that the belief "I am worthless and unlovable" is running your life. On the other hand, if you have had positive experiences in life you will have positive ideas about yourself. You might believe "I am smart and successful." In this case, the same holds true; this belief, "I am smart and successful," will be reflected in your outward experience. In fact, you can change your life completely by simply ignoring your past and changing what you believe about yourself.

You have an opportunity to see beyond any belief when you simply *stop* believing everything you think for just one moment. It is in this moment of *stopping* that you have an opportunity to see what is deeper, what is pure, what has no problem with your story. It is completely free from all your beliefs. This place is like no other and you can find it in the very core of your being, in the depths of your heart. This is where you want to focus your attention in order to recognize that you are eternally free. It is from this place of pure awareness that divine, mystical Truth emerges. This Truth is the primary reason that divine scripture has remained intact for centuries. There is a transmission of Grace that transcends belief, that transcends all thought. This pure, radiant transmission of Grace bypasses the mind completely, entering into the pure awareness of the heart. All the great religions emerged essentially from a direct experience of this pure divine awareness.

Buddha, Jesus, Moses, and Muhammad all had a direct, unknowable experience of pure Grace. There was clarity about them; what they shared with others transcended the accepted beliefs of their time. Jesus, for example, did something that had never been done before. He brought divine Truth from the realm of scholars, philosophers, and religious clerics and gave it to the poor common man. He spoke of everyday things like mustard seeds and wine to help the average, uneducated person understand the eternal Truth that he was pointing to. He left the religion of his parents to point to something deeper, something pure, a purity that transcended what was known and unknown. Buddha also experienced That which language only dances on the surface of. He recognized the pure seeingness that flows above, below, and through all words, experiences, and beliefs.

Muhammad experienced the divine embrace of the Angel Gabriel, whose transmission of Grace has evolved into Islam, one of the world's largest religions. Even the word *Islam* points directly to freedom. It has a dual meaning: surrender and peace. The deeper meaning is based in the Truth that through surrender to Allah (God), you will be guided to the abode of Peace. As it states in the Quran, the Holy Book of Islam, *"Allah invites us all to the abode of peace and He guides him who wishes to be guided in the exact right path leading to the goal."* Moses met the unknowable pure Grace of God, I am that I am, in the silence of Mount Sinai. This pure Grace enabled him to free an enslaved people and become a prominent religious figure in both Judaism and Christianity. People from all different walks of life are inexplicably drawn to the purity of the divine consciousness that people like Jesus, Buddha, Moses, and Muhammad demonstrate. These are the people who had the courage to transcend their own personal beliefs and the beliefs of society, to stay true to the purest possible message of Grace, and to bring forward a deeper truth to others.

The word *religion* evolved from the Latin word *religio*, which means to re-tie us to God, like a ligament ties a muscle to bone. It is centered in the belief in a higher power or governor of the Universe. Religion emerged from the core belief that we are all separate from God, further propagating the egoic idea that this "higher" power is not here, so it must be somewhere else. At its core, religion is a set of beliefs that offer a teaching, practice, or method to reunite us with this higher power. Or it is based in the belief that God is an all-powerful person who is separate from you. Many religions can be traced back to the beliefs that emerged from the life experience of a single individual or group of individuals. From these beliefs, rituals, religious dogma, and spiritual practice evolved to help guide others into a deeper understanding of the divine mystical Grace that is at the core of every religion.

Religion is rooted in belief, which lives in the realm of the mind, which is past and centered on the story of the people who experienced divine Truth. Over time, the seeds of truth that began a religion can become clouded by beliefs based on *concepts* of truth and not the Truth itself. Throughout history, religion has been used as a strategy to end suffering, avoid hell, or ensure passage into heaven or nirvana. However, if you approach the divine truth of any religion with the idea, "what will I get from this?" desire is already present. Desire by its very nature says, "I do not have it and I want it," creating an immediate separation from Truth. Once desire emerges, what attracted you to religion or spiritual practices has been polluted by the desire for something. This objectifies the pure truth that the teaching offers and renders it ineffective and lifeless. As long as there is a thread of desire intertwined with your spiritual practice, suffering will continue.

Pure divine mystical Grace, the seed of Truth that is alive in all religions, is what draws people to religion. Whether or not you are drawn to religion, there is a deep longing for freedom in the very core of your bones. It is this longing that drives you outward toward the fulfillment of worldly desire or inward toward the fulfillment of spiritual desire. Whether it is a worldly or spiritual desire, when you let go of the idea "what will I get from this?" there is a natural opening that occurs. From this opening, Truth can be received heart to heart, core-to-core. If religion or spiritual practice becomes a formula to give you what you want, it is already polluted; it has become a method for what you need to *do* in order to get what you want. As Papaji said, it is *"reading the menu."* When you focus on your *intellectual* method for getting Truth, the deeper meaning is lost. Many people experience this as a kind of deadness, and turn away from religion, thinking that it is the religion or spiritual practice that is ineffective. However, it is only what you *think* and what you believe religion will *do for you* that renders the teaching ineffective. As Buddha points out: *"The source of all suffering is desire and must be abandoned."*

Throughout history there are examples of people who remained pure: Buddha, Jesus, Saint John of the Cross, Mother Theresa, Saint Francis of Assisi, the Dalai Lama, Amachi, Gurumayi, and of course the beloved Ramana. By pure, I do not mean they were better than you; they simply were devoted to God, the Self. They did not have the "mecentric" idea, "if I am devoted, what will I get?" Through their devotion to the Truth, which cannot be touched by desire, Truth revealed itself to them.

You can feel the difference when you are in the presence of someone who has recognized the Truth that lives beyond belief. It is not just what Saint Francis of Assisi or Ramana did or said that drew people to them. The Truth is not revealed by just their speech or actions; it is revealed by the transmission of Love and Grace that permeates their entire being. You can literally feel your heart open in the presence of an enlightened master or saint. This is one of the key reasons they are remembered: It was the transmission of pure Love that emanated from them that deeply touched the hearts of those who came into their presence. This is the core reason that these people have not been forgotten, as well as the reason that, in many cases, their words have become sacred scripture. People were transformed by their presence and lifted beyond the limitations of the body-mind experience.

This life-transforming transmission has been written about and talked about for centuries. Ramana was silent for many years, but people still gathered around him in the hope of being transformed by the energy that was emanating from him. Because of the numerous reports of the miraculous abilities that clear conscious people have, average people mistakenly think that if they act a certain way, they, too, will be able to demonstrate these miraculous abilities. It is not uncommon for people to subjugate themselves to hours and hours of rigorous spiritual practice in the vain hope that they will be like the Buddha, Jesus, or Krishna.

Enlightenment takes on a new meaning because of this mysterious transmission of Love that emanates from the great teachers of Truth. These concepts about enlightenment became objectified by the ego (I-thought) into the common belief that it was only for the most holy of holy people, or that it could be attained only after years and years of spiritual practice. In other words, people began to develop beliefs about enlightenment based on the idea, "Enlightenment is somewhere else and I have to *do* something in order to get it," or even the idea, "Once I am enlightened, my life will transform into perfection and everything will be wonderful."

The same holds true for freedom. There have been many different beliefs about what freedom is. To the average person, freedom usually means, "I can do what I want, when I want, where I want," or "I can get whatever I want." Can you see how the ego, the I-thought, has slipped in here?

Freedom, like enlightenment, has been objectified into something that must be sought after, something to get or hold onto. Beliefs such as "once I am free, my life will be perfect," or "if I go to church, I will be purified; I will be a good person" cloud the Truth of what enlightenment and freedom are.

Ultimately, any belief is a barrier to freedom. All beliefs are deeply rooted in the I-thought. This I-thought immediately separates you from the freedom that you are seeking. It represents either a conscious or an unconscious belief in the idea that "I am not good enough to be enlightened," or "There is something I must *do*, a spiritual practice or prayer that will deliver me to freedom." This separation and objectification of freedom drives you outward toward the object desired.

Once freedom becomes objectified it has transformed into the idea that it is a thing that lives outside of you. It becomes something that you must find or something to attain in order to be happy. Freedom from this point of view implies that you are not free, that you are in bondage and you must *do* something in order to free yourself.

What is it that binds you? Bondage emerges from the ego, which is the root of desire and the source of your belief that you separate from the freedom you are seeking. The ego is a powerful bond that is irrevocably linked to the body and the three aspects of mind (I-thoughts, I-feelings, and I-sensations). The experience of separation caused by the ego is also the source of the objectification of freedom. It stems from the core belief that freedom is not here, so it must be somewhere else. This belief further strengthens the sense of separation and is the reason that you start to look for something that cannot be found, creating a never-ending cycle of seeking,

seeking, seeking or practicing, practicing, practicing. From this perspective, freedom is always just beyond reach.

If freedom is not an object and it is not somewhere else, what and where is it? Freedom is not a strategy for ensuring that your life will be perfect, holy, or somehow better. When you have a belief about what freedom is or what it will give you, this belief acts as a barrier to the freedom you are seeking. It blinds you to what is already here, right now. The idea that "freedom is not here so it must be somewhere else" is by its very nature rooted in desire or the idea, "I do not have it and I want to get it." Remember, beliefs are bundles of thoughts that live in mind, which emerges from the primal I-thought. Any belief you identify with acts as a container of thought. The more you identify with these containers of thought the more real you perceive them to be. This identification makes it very difficult to see That which is free from all beliefs. The objectification of freedom and your desire to attain it impede your ability to see what is already here – That which is so close, even closer than your own breath!

Any belief can create a false image in mind. It is like a mirage in the desert – you see it, but you can never reach it, or drink the water to satisfy your thirst. For example, based on descriptions of Buddha's state of happiness once he realized the state of nirvana, you might think that you have to be happy in order to attain that state. Or you might believe that you should always be happy once you have become enlightened. If you have this belief about enlightenment, you might try to become happy by practicing meditation. If you reach a state of happiness, suffering sets in when you have the desire to maintain this state. Once you have the desire to hold onto happiness, you have once again returned to the state of unhappiness, simply because desire by its very nature moves your awareness outward away from the source of happiness. You might even attempt to create the state of nirvana by *doing* happiness instead of allowing the state of happiness to naturally emerge. All of these efforts emerge from your belief that you are the *doer* and that you have to *do* something to attain enlightenment. It is this belief in this non-existent *doer* that fuels your desire to attain the happiness that enlightenment promises. In Truth, all of your beliefs and desires only dance around the Truth, becoming a huge barrier to recognizing your own freedom. All of your thoughts, images, feelings, and experiences come and go; they simply do not last. Your feelings and experiences constantly change in relationship to the words, feelings, and images that you are identified with. Freedom is independent of any thought, feeling, experience, or state of consciousness; it is always present in states of both happiness and unhappiness.

What is present when you are happy and when you are not? What is constant and unchanging, free from the story of you, unaffected by emotions, beliefs, attachments, and desires? Belief will transform into a gateway when you simply drop all of your beliefs just for one moment. It is in this moment of stopping that you have an opportunity to open to a new way of understanding which will reveal something that all beliefs hide. This is what Jesus was pointing to when he said, *"Know the Truth and the Truth will make you Free."* He did not say *you* will make *you* free; he did not even say that he would set you free. He said the *Truth* will make you free; there is *no doing* on your part. Truth reveals itself to you naturally when you stop following your thoughts outward and instead look to see where all thoughts emerge. There is no doing to get; there is simply a stopping to recognize what is already here, regardless of your story, your experiences, your beliefs, your attachments, or your desires. Only when you *stop* completely in this way do you have the opportunity to see this for yourself. It is the recognition of the Self that is possible when you *stop* that leads to the recognition of your eternal freedom. Recognition of the Truth can only be revealed when you *stop* and face the unknowable Self – That which is free from all of it.

This is what Buddha, Jesus, and Ramana are all pointing to: the great eternal presence that is alive within you. This freedom is in you and all around you. It is the indescribable all-knowing Self that will reveal itself when you *stop*, when you allow yourself to be still and quiet, when you are willing to surrender and drop all of your beliefs for just a moment. Most importantly, when you are willing to let go of everything you think you know, it is then and only then that you will recognize what you have always been, what you are, and always will be. You will recognize that you are freedom itself. You must even drop your concepts of the unknown, or what God or the Self is. Let it all go and surrender! What are you waiting for? Stop right now and see for yourself that this is Truth itself! What ever you believe will be your truth, your reality. Whatever you believe will actually create that experience for you. Your beliefs can open the gateway of freedom or slam it shut. It is up to you to decide. (Sound familiar?)

Any thought commands tremendous power to either free you or trap you. The great enlightened masters all have one thing in common: They *stopped* and surrendered to the vast emptiness of the Self. In that *stopping* they transcended the thoughts and beliefs that were blinding them from the Truth. In that moment of *stopping,* they recognized their own eternal nature. Once you *stop,* once you are still and quiet, you have an opportunity to recognize this for yourself. Then the pure Grace of the Self will reveal your natural state of being-consciousness-bliss. Other than stopping, there is literally no doing on your part. Being-consciousness-bliss is the freedom that you really are; it is dancing under the surface of your beliefs. You will naturally feel its alive, pure, conscious presence the moment you recognize it within your own heart!

If you still find that you are not recognizing this presence, check and see what words, thoughts, or feelings you are focused on, and simply *stop* focusing on them. This is what is meant by letting go of your story and your beliefs. Stopping simply means to stop giving your attention to them and instead focus all your awareness at the source.

Letting go can seem to be a scary thing. You might be thinking, "Let go of my beliefs? Let go of my story, my past? Who would I be without my story?" This fear can lead you into the core of your being. What is fear, really, and how can it be a gateway to freedom?

Fear

When you allow yourself to contemplate the letting go of your story, it is natural to experience fear. It could be the fear of non-existence, the fear that your life has been meaningless, the fear of losing something, or simply the fear of the unknown. The origin of fear can be found in your identification with your body or the idea "I am the body," which emerges from the primal I-thought or ego. The primary purpose of the ego is to ensure the survival of the body. When the survival of the body or *perceived* survival of the body is threatened, the natural reaction is fear. Fear is a powerful energy that is filtered through the I-thoughts, I-feelings, and I-sensations of your mind, causing you to avoid anything you perceive to be a threat to the body or who you perceive yourself to be.

The ego depends on the body for survival. It is from the ego that the idea "I am the body" emerges. Since the primary purpose of the ego is the survival of the body, death of the body is the deepest fear of the ego. This primal fear of death is the force behind many different conscious and unconscious strategies for survival. These strategies live in your mind to protect the body from any potential danger. It is, in effect, a warning system that lets you know that you must avoid walking in front of a moving bus in order to prevent injury or death of your body. There is absolutely nothing wrong with the ego or the mind from the perspective that they ensure that you are protected from potentially dangerous situations. It is only when this natural protective nature turns into a strategy for avoidance that fear is transformed into a powerful barrier to freedom.

Since fear of physical death is rooted in the ego, the primal fear is that of non-existence. This is the primary reason that the end of your story can be perceived to be very frightening. Your identification with your story creates a very deep belief that your story is who you are. When the story disappears you think that you will disappear, too; that you will be non-existent. Ultimately, it is not the fear of the unknown that is frightening; it is the fear of leaving what you know or leaving your past. Letting go of your past can be scary because it is so familiar. Even if you have a horrific past, you still cling to it simply because you are comfortable with what you have known.

Holding onto your story is an attempt to maintain some sense of identity or maintain what you feel comfortable with. The primal fear of non-existence, rooted in survival of the body, acts as a powerful force that causes you to remain attached to your story. In truth, only the body and the story die. Who you are, beyond the body, beyond your story, is eternal and never dies. To discover this truth for yourself is to meet death completely, in this moment, by inquiring, "Who is it who dies?" This inquiry led Ramana into the deepest discovery of Truth, changing his life and the lives of those who meet him. This single inquiry can awaken your consciousness to the truth of *Being* – beyond ego, mind, time, attachment, desire, belief, and fear.

Not only is there a fear of non-existence; there can also be a fear of losing something, losing your mind, or going crazy. What would your life mean without your past? What would happen if you lost your mind? It is only when you are attached to something that the fear of losing it arises. Both mind and ego are attached to the body, so fear of losing your mind arises from your deep attachment to your body. From the body-mind perspective there is a sense of duality – the idea "I am separate from everything and everyone else." Where there is duality there is desire, anger, hatred, jealousy, and greed, which is simply madness. Supreme peace arises when you recognize that no-mind is sanity. At its core all fear is based on the idea of "other" separate from everything, which emerges from the ego or the idea "I am this body." When you recognize that this "other" is non-existent, then there is no fear, no mind, no ego, no body, and no story. All that remains is a peace that surpasses all understanding. All fear vanishes when you recognize the infinite Self within your own heart, the very core of your being. This Self cannot be held onto and it can never be lost, so in Truth there is absolutely nothing to fear.

You could be wondering, "How can fear help me find the freedom that I am seeking?" Since fear is rooted in survival of the body, the protective nature of the mind causes you to avoid anything that you are afraid of. This avoidance becomes a strategy for survival. When fear is avoided it is a barrier to freedom. Fear will transform into a gateway to freedom when you allow your consciousness to penetrate any fear you have and tell the truth about it. Freedom asks that you be ruthlessly honest with yourself. If you want to be free, you must tell yourself the truth about what you are afraid of. Most people do not want to be this honest with themselves. It is simply too scary, so we choose to avoid anything uncomfortable and we *especially* avoid anything that we are deeply afraid of.

Avoiding or resisting any fear requires a great deal of energy, and acts only to strengthen your fears. When you tell the truth to yourself and meet your fears instead of avoiding them, you have an opportunity to fully experience them. Like desire, once you fully meet any fear by not acting it out and not suppressing it, the fear itself transforms into a sacred fire. Once you enter the sacred fire of fear, the emptiness of fear will reveal itself to you. Meeting your deepest fears simply releases you from the grip of fear, which frees you from all of your conscious and unconscious strategies to avoid it.

Your story and all your strategies to avoid fear are simply layers upon layers that hide the Truth. You have the choice to be honest and meet your fears, to lie to yourself, or to create a new strategy to avoid your fears. When there is no-mind there are no options. There are no options in Truth; options exist only in your mind as strategies for survival. Once you meet your fears all of your strategies fall away revealing the eternal silence that is always present, never absent.

Anything you avoid has some form of fear at its very core. This is worth repeating: *Anything you avoid has some form of fear at its very core.* You have an opportunity to free yourself from your fears once you are ruthlessly honest with yourself and fully meet them. Fear lives in the mind, which is past and ultimately does not exist. Your mind operates so quickly that you can be completely unconscious that you have any fear. In other words, you have lived with fear so long that it has become part of who you think yourself to be.

Take a moment right now and allow yourself to locate any feeling of fear that you have in your body. You might experience fear in your throat, chest, head, or the pit of your stomach. Once you have found this feeling in your body, focus your awareness directly into your fear and allow your consciousness to penetrate all of the thoughts, feelings, and images that are associated with this fear. Just as a matter of investigation in this moment, allow yourself to discover what is really there at the core of this fear. For example, when you locate fear in your body, you might notice the thought, "I am afraid of being alone." Focus all of your awareness on the thought associated with the fear. Allow yourself to fully experience this fear without acting it out or suppressing it. Initially, you might feel the fear rising up within your body. You might meet the "edge" of this fear and feel yourself pulling back. If you find yourself pulling back, push deeper into the core of this fear. Do not move to suppress or to act out this feeling; simply penetrate it with your consciousness. When you do not move, fear transforms into a sacred fire that burns away all feelings, thoughts, and images, revealing the living Truth within you. When you stop moving, this sacred fire consumes everything.

Instead of meeting fear in this way, most people usually *do* all kinds of things to avoid the fears that they have, which makes it impossible to recognize that you are already free. If you are either consciously or unconsciously avoiding fear, you are expending a great deal of energy, trying to avoid whatever it is that you are afraid of. Avoidance causes your life force to be drained away while strengthening your fear. By avoiding fear, you reinforce your belief that fear is real. You are literally trapped in the fear-based thoughts, images and feelings, which live only in the mind. For example, the thought "I am afraid to die" is a very powerful fear that is fueled by the thought, "I am this body." The more you avoid these thoughts the more strength they gain.

If you are ruthlessly honest with yourself and fully meet whatever fear you have, including the fear of death, you will see for yourself that at the core of any fear is no-thing. As Buddha discovered, *"Form is emptiness and emptiness is form."* Fear is completely void of anything; like penetrating a bubble, there is nothing inside. If you continue to avoid your fears, these thoughts, which are "no-thing," become a very powerful "thing" that is literally draining the energy out of your life. What is amazing is that you are spending a great deal of energy to avoid something that is not even real! If you do not believe this, just take a moment to check it out. What is at the very core of any fear that you have? Look and see. It is so incredibly freeing to take a moment, just a moment, to contemplate the Truth of this.

You have a chance right now to change your life forever. If you haven't already, take a moment right this minute to penetrate your deepest fear. Stay with the thoughts, feelings, and images associated with this fear, until fear reveals its emptiness to you. If you feel yourself wanting to pull away from it, just allow your consciousness to further penetrate the thoughts, feelings, and images that emerge into your mind. If another fear emerges, allow your consciousness to sink into whatever appears until you get to the very core of it. What do you notice about the fear when you have fully met it at its core? You will discover that there is only empty silence there—a peace that surpasses understanding. The moment you fully meet any fear there is an instant when your mind naturally stops, allowing you to recognize this silent presence. In the absence of thought, meaning, or associated feeling, fear is experienced as an emptiness or vibration. Meeting fear allows you to relax completely and rest in this emptiness. The cost of continuing to avoid fear is significant. It requires a great deal of effort, and it literally blocks you from your natural state, which is being-consciousness-bliss.   Avoidance of fear causes your life force to be steadily drained away, which leads to either conscious or unconscious suffering.

If you are having trouble meeting fear, you can follow the words associated with the fear to their source by thinking backwards. In other words, if you are afraid of being alone you can think backwards starting with the last word *alone,* then moving backwards to the next word *be*, and the next *to*, then *afraid* then the next *am* and finally the first word *I*. Do you see how we have come full circle here? What comes before the thought "I?" This is a useful technique that can help you to see clearly the pure conscious awareness that all thoughts and all fears emerge from and return to. (A word of caution here: Any method, technique, or practice can be rendered ineffective the moment it becomes a strategy to get something. It is useful only when you approach it with an open heart and mind, free from expectations.)

When you stop for a moment to see what comes before the thought "I" you will see for yourself the indescribable, infinite ocean of the Self that you are. The Self is the Cosmos, beyond the body, beyond your story, beyond who you think yourself to be. This ocean of the Self is where all thought emerges from and returns to. This is where you want to focus all your awareness. The root of all suffering can be found in your identification with words, images, and feelings. The moment you stop acting on or suppressing them is the moment you will no longer suffer. In this eternal moment you will be free to see something that is much deeper: the ocean of bliss from which all thoughts, images, and feelings arise.

It is so simple. If you no longer want to suffer, stop believing in the words, images, and feelings that you are having for just one moment! As Gangaji once said, *"Truth is simple and cannot be practiced."* The moment that you *stop* attaching to or identifying with the words, images, and feelings that appear in mind, they will transform into a gateway to freedom.

Fear can be either a gateway or a barrier to freedom. (This must really be sounding familiar by now!) If you are not willing to meet your fears, you will be bound by your strategies to avoid fear and remain with what is comfortable. This is a false comfort, and ultimately will lead only to more suffering. To release yourself from any fear, fear asks that you have the courage to meet it in this moment. In the end, the choice is yours. Are you going to let fear be a barrier or a gateway to freedom?

To be free from fear is to face it and see what is there, to dive directly into it! If you have not tried it already, you really can do this now. Please take a moment and write down on a piece of paper your greatest fear. Hold it in front of you until you get a real sense of the fear that this thought evokes within you. Locate where you feel that fear in your body and dive right into the core of it, completely immersing yourself in it. Stay with it. If you feel yourself pulling away, close your eyes and dive even deeper. If you stay with this long enough you will discover that there is nothing there; nothing, nothing, nothing.

You might be willing to meet your fears and stop identifying with the words, images, and feelings that are appearing in this moment, but you might still be wondering, "How do I let go of my story?" The answer lies in the deepest surrender. What does "surrender" mean and why is it important (in fact, crucial) to recognizing your own freedom?

Surrender

Surrender at its core means to surrender your story. The moment you surrender your story you let go of the idea of you, the ego, from which all stories emerge. When the story is gone, your ego vanishes naturally, and all that remains is your physical form, empty of any identity – naked, vulnerable, and mortal. Remember, there is no story without the ego and there is no story without a past. Surrender simply enables you to meet the emptiness of the story and the physical body, which someday will be consumed by death. Your body has a beginning (birth), a middle (life) and an end (death). Anything that has a beginning, middle, and end is transitory, not permanent. Like thoughts, feelings, and images, the ego, your story, and even your body are constantly changing. They all emerge from and return to the ocean of the

Self. The Self does not have a beginning, middle, or end; it is eternal and unknowable.

Through surrender, you come face to face with death. Since this meeting of death is horrifying, it is much easier to think of surrender as something to *do*, which is actually a strategy to keep busy so you can avoid meeting death. When you give it all up and *become* surrender, there is an opportunity to fully meet your own mortality, which will reveal That which never dies. As Jesus said, *"Whosoever shall seek to save his life shall lose it; and whosoever shall lose his life shall preserve it."* By meeting your own death you see That which is eternal – the vast ocean of the Self within you.

Papaji often used the ocean as an analogy to illustrate the Truth of this. You know that waves emerge from the ocean and return to the ocean. When a wave emerges from the ocean it forgets that it *is* the ocean.

Similarly, when you are born into this world, you emerge from the source of all consciousness – the Self – and you forget that you are this Self. The wave is always the ocean and you are always the Self. The wave is never separate from the ocean, just as you are never separate from the Self. The wave emerges from and returns to the ocean, as you emerge from and return to the Self.

To illustrate the merging quality of surrender, Papaji also used the analogy of a salt doll that is thrown into the ocean. What happens to the salt doll once it meets the ocean? Well, of course, it dissolves into the ocean. Nothing remains of what was once the salt doll. Once you meet the Self, like the salt doll dissolving into the ocean, you merge with the Self. As you merge with the Self, nothing remains of what you once thought of as yourself. From the perspective of the ego, this might be a very scary thought (e.g., "What happens to me?"). From the perspective of the Self, there never was a "me" in the first place. The "me" that you identify with as "you" is your body and the story about your life in that body. Surrender is a gateway to recognizing that you are not your body, that you are eternally free, you are in fact freedom itself. This is true enlightenment, the recognition of who you really are.

Freedom invites you to tell the Truth. Can you give up everything you think you know? Are you ready to release everything you worked so hard to attain? Are you willing to meet your own physical death? Surrender can be perceived as difficult primarily because of your sense of "doer-ship" and "owner-ship." You perceive yourself to be the *doer* ("I am this person doing this thing.") In addition, you think of yourself as the *owner* ("I worked so hard to get this, it is mine!") True surrender requires no doing and there is no ownership. When you surrender, your mind naturally turns toward its source; and just as the salt doll disappears into the ocean, this non-existent *doer* vanishes into the Self! If there is no *doer,* then obviously there is nothing to own or cling to. When you release your concept of being the *doer,* you are free to notice something much deeper. You are free to *see the seer.*

Just for a moment, drop your name, story, desires, attachments, concepts, and beliefs. When all this is gone, what remains? In surrender, you simply allow yourself to merge with what is always present: the infinite ocean of the Self, which is hidden only by your story. Surrender is a letting go of everything so the Self can reveal. It is peace itself.

Jesus said, *"You are the light of the world,"* pointing to the truth of who you are beyond your story. The statement, *"You are the light of the world*," illuminates the Truth that no matter what your frame of reference, no matter what your story, you are the one constant *light* which is the Self or God. The Self is the one constant force in the universe. Regardless of your story or frame of reference, the moment you surrender, you are free to see that which never changes, the infinite light of the Self. You will recognize that who you are is this never ending light!

To be crystal clear, let us take a moment to look at what the Self is *not*: The Self is <u>not</u> a feeling or emotion; it is <u>not</u> an experience (no matter how profound or spiritual an experience might be); it is <u>not</u> a thought, idea or belief; and it is <u>not</u> a state of consciousness. Words are grossly inadequate in describing the Self. The Self *is* emptiness. The word that most accurately describes the Self is *nothing* or *no-thing* – The Self <u>is</u> the substratum of all existence; thoughts, images, feelings all dance on the surface of the infinite Self. It is omniscient. It cannot be attained. It can only be recognized.

Surrender is necessary to recognize the Truth of who you are. It requires that you allow yourself to turn toward the Self, by stopping everything and turning your attention to the Source of all thought. To see the Self is to see the *seer*. This is the core of this teaching: See the *seer* beyond name and form. As Papaji points out, *"Name and form hide reality."* When you recognize the seer beyond name and form – *the infinite one that is looking through your eyes* – you will see that which cannot be seen; the infinite light of the Self.

The Self is free from the limitations of the mind. It works in all dimensions simultaneously. It is omnipresent. It is beyond the ability of mind to fully comprehend the eternal nature of Self. The

Self is the pure consciousness that enables you to see with your heart. Your eyes by themselves do not see; they are only lenses that open and close based on the amount of light in your environment. If the eye is just a lens, then who is looking through the lens? Or as Papaji once asked, *"What is before the retina of your eye?"*

Once you fully recognize the Self, there is a complete *absence of doubt*, an unshakeable certainty or pure faith. If you have doubt, there is absolutely nothing to do to get rid of it. Doubt naturally falls away when you allow yourself to stop and find the source of the doubter. As Ramana so eloquently states, *"There is no use in removing doubts. If we clear one doubt, another rises and there will be no end of doubts. All doubts will cease, only when the doubter and his source have been found. Seek the source of the doubter, and you will find that he is really non-existent. Doubter ceasing, doubts will cease."*

We often make the mistake of thinking doubt is questioning, but questioning is open; if you are questioning, you are open to finding an answer. Doubting, on the other hand, is closed; when you doubt something, you are skeptical, which blocks you from receiving an answer. Doubt appears to be real, but is it? Papaji once said, *"Doubt is the illusionary wall between you and freedom."* Doubt transforms into a gateway to freedom when you stop for a moment and doubt the doubter. ("Who is it who doubts?") Once you let go all the way and surrender, or see the source of the doubter, you will recognize that there is no doubter. If there is no doubter, then obviously there will be an *absence of doubt*. This is the key: *Doubting the doubter*, you will know without a doubt the Truth of the Self within you. You will know that you are the Self, the Cosmos.

Surrender is one of the most sacred gifts of enlightenment. It represents the great way of freedom, or the middle path that the Buddha pointed to. The moment you surrender you will see for yourself the great ocean of bliss that you are, and your desire to hold onto your story will naturally fall away. Surrender is the key that opens the sacred gateway of the heart! Once this gateway opens, you will move through it the moment that you stop and are still and quiet.

You might be wondering, "Stop to move? What does that mean?" Surrender is meeting death. When you meet death, you have an opportunity to move or to stop and become aware of That which never moves. As strange as it might seem, meeting death reveals the *essential question* that unlocks the mystery of the "great way" of enlightenment.

What is this *essential question,* and why is it important?

The Essential Question

To most of us, death represents an end. However, for a small boy in Southern India named Venkataraman ("Ramana" for short), death was the beginning of a journey into consciousness that revealed the *essential question*. By meeting his fear of death, Ramana awoke to the truth of *being* known as enlightenment by asking a simple yet *essential question*. Ramana explained what happened:

"One day I was alone on the first floor of my uncle's house; I was in my usual state of health. But a sudden unmistakable fear of death seized me. I felt I was going to die. Why I should have so felt cannot now be explained by anything felt in the body. I did not, however, trouble myself to discover if the fear was well grounded. I did not care to consult doctors or elders or even friends. I felt I had to solve the problem myself then and there.

The actual inquiry and discovery of "Who am I?" was over on the very first day, after a short time. Instinctively, I held my breath and began to dive inward with my inquiry into my own nature. I stretched myself like a corpse, and it seemed to me that my body had actually become rigid – 'I' was not dead – 'I' was, on the other hand, conscious of being alive, in existence. So the question arose in me, "What is this 'I'?" I felt that it was a force or current working despite the rigidity or activity of the body, though existing in connection with it. It was that current or force or center that constituted my personality, that kept me acting, moving, etc... The fear of death dropped off. I was absorbed in the contemplation of that current."

By meeting his own death, Ramana discovered the *essential question* that provides the most direct path to freedom. He discovered that by diving into himself and inquiring, *"Who am 'I'? What is this 'I'?"* he immediately recognized the source of all thought. Self-inquiry is Ramana's sacred gift of enlightenment. It requires no doing. By stopping, being still, being silent, and diving into his fear of death, the fear dropped off. Ramana became absorbed in the contemplation of That "current" from which the I-thought emerged. This absorption in That which comes before the thought "I" will lead you directly to the source of all thought, the Self.

S*topping, silence, and surrender* occur naturally through Self-inquiry. Self-inquiry represents an invitation to stop everything for just one moment and ask yourself the question, "Who am I?" It is not an intellectual exercise. Any answer your mind can give is *not* the answer. Even the most sublime answer such as, "I am one with the Universe," is only the mind attempting to describe what is indescribable. When you deeply contemplate the question "Who am I?"

and ignore any answer that arises, your mind will at some point naturally stop and invert to its source. In that moment, your mind will fall silent. Once the mind stops, you will naturally recognize the source of all thought. You do not have to *do* something to *get* something. (Surely, by now this concept is *very* familiar!) If you are trying to get something on any level, then desire has crept in, blocking you from the recognition that you already have That which you have been seeking. If you find that your thoughts become very active, do not *do* anything; simply stop touching them. Do not be troubled by your thoughts; simply notice them. Thoughts are like children at play: They are in constant motion, emerging from and disappearing into the infinite. Focus your attention on where your thoughts come from and where they return, and you will merge with the ocean of the Self.

Jesus, Buddha, and Ramana have one thing in common: All three of them stopped, and in that stopping, the infinite Self revealed itself. To experience this, I invite you to put down this book for a moment, close your eyes, and allow yourself to be still, to be silence itself. Once you are quiet, allow yourself to contemplate your own death. Ask yourself: *Who is it who dies?* Focus all your attention on your heart and ask yourself the questions: *Who am I? What is this "I"?* Stop to see where it comes from. If the thought "I am me" emerges, go deeper – go beyond the I-thought. (Remember, there is no intellectual answer to this question.) Give yourself permission to experience That which lives beyond identity. Inquire deeply into what is present before the thought "I." Stop for just a moment to see the seer. This process does not require much time. The Truth can reveal itself in a fraction of a second.

It is important to emphasize again that none of this requires any *doing* on your part. At this point you must release your sense of *doer-ship* and allow the Self to naturally reveal itself to you. You are the observer as well as that which is being observed. Look at this observer. *Who is this observer, this seer?*

Once you recognize the Self, you will understand why it is not a feeling or experience. Feelings and experiences come and go. They emerge from the Self, but they are *not* the Self. If you desire freedom, there will be a moment when the lens of your mind inverts on its own, enabling you to see clearly to the source. This is the *essential shift* of Self-inquiry; it is a transmission of Grace that transcends all knowledge. The moment you recognize the Self, beyond what you *think* it is, you will recognize the freedom and joy of your true nature. A word of caution here: The *feelings* that arise from this *essential shift* might not last. The desire to hold onto these feelings is a trap of the mind. Remember, the Self is not a feeling or experience. Once you have the glimpse into the infinite nature of the Self, you will know that it is constant, always present. It will never leave you. How can it leave you, when the Self is who you are?

Self-inquiry is the most direct path of seeing the seer – the infinite Self. It is the path of knowledge Gnana (divine wisdom), as well as Bhakti (love and devotion). As Ramana explained, *"The eternal, unbroken, natural state of abiding in the Self is Gnana. To abide in the Self you must love the Self. Since God is in fact the Self, love of the Self is love of God, and that is Bhakti."* Self-inquiry (divine wisdom) is abidance in the Self, and abidance in the Self (devotion) is divine love. When Jesus was asked what the two greatest commandments were, he responded, *"You shall love the Lord your God with all your heart, and with all your soul and with all your mind. This is the great and foremost commandment. And the second is like it – You shall love your neighbor as yourself."* Notice how he says with *all* your heart, *all* your soul, and *all* your mind. When you focus your entire being (heart, soul, and mind) on God, the Truth will naturally reveal itself. With this single statement he is pointing you to freedom. He is letting you know that through devotion, there will be a natural emergence of the divine love and wisdom of the Self. Once this divine love emerges, you will recognize the same infinite Self within everyone; then you will naturally *love everyone as your Self.*

Only the ego thinks, "I must *do* to get or maintain." Remember, there is no *doing.* There is no way of doing something to get the Self or keep the Self. The Self simply is always present. This is what Jesus meant when he said, *"I am with you always."* He meant God, "I am that I am," pure Being, is with you always. Once you recognize the Self, you will know without a doubt that enlightenment is not an experience or a feeling. Experiences and feelings change constantly. The Self never changes; it is always constant. It is present whether you are happy or unhappy. Once you have glimpsed the infinite Self, you will naturally feel devotion to this pure conscious presence and you will know without a doubt, on a much deeper and intimate level, that you are eternal.

As you awaken to your eternal nature, all the ghosts and demons of your deepest fears will come to greet you. No worries! When they come, just wave and say hello, face them, dive deep into them, and you will discover that they really are nothing. This might not be easy for you. The ego is very powerful and its primary purpose is to insure the survival of the body. It will start to play all kinds of tricks, even using the "glimpse" of the infinite to trap or trick you. This is the ego fighting for survival. Even after you recognize the Truth, you must continue to walk the razor's edge, remaining aware of the tricks of the ego. Just because you have seen the Self does not mean that you will experience joy and bliss forever. No. No. No. Remember, the Self is constant, like light. It is not an emotion. It does not change; it has no form; it is emptiness itself. Since you are in a physical body you are subject to the thoughts and emotions of the body. The second that you identify with any thought, it will pull you back into the experience of the mind or the past, with all its associated emotions. Ultimately, it is your choice.

It is possible to remain in a state of bliss, as Ramana did. Once he experienced the depth and peace of the Self, he *chose* to focus his awareness on the Self and nothing else. Through this absorption in the Self, he remained in silence for many years. Ramana's profound silence was so pure that hundreds of people came just to sit in his presence. His form became a channel of pure consciousness, divine wisdom, and love. The Grace that emanated from Ramana responded directly to faith of those who sought their eternal freedom at his feet. As a result, many people who were devoted to God awoke to the Self just by sitting quietly in Ramana's presence. If you remain absorbed in the Self, you will also experience the supreme silence of being-consciousness-bliss, (*sat-chit-ananda*), which emanated from Ramana during his life and continues to emanate after his physical death.

Please be careful here: You do not want to fall into the trap of trying to be like Ramana. Remaining absorbed in the Self is what occurred naturally for him; this might or might not occur for you. It is enough to remember that recognizing the Self does not necessarily mean that you will remain in a blissful state. Feelings, thoughts, and images will continue to appear in your mind, just as they did prior to recognizing the Self, but they will no longer have the power over you that they once had. You will simply notice the emptiness of them as they emerge from and return to the Self. You will recognize that they are not real.

Self-inquiry strikes at the root of all thoughts, feelings, and images that emerge in mind. Through Self-inquiry, the mind naturally becomes absorbed in the Self. Absorption in the Self can result in what is known as *nirvikalpa samadhi*, which is a blissful, trance-like state. As profoundly deep as the *nirvikalpa samadhi* state is, it will not last. This is simply because even after the Self is realized, or a state of *nirvikalpa samadhi* is achieved, the ego and mind still retain tremendous power. Ramana often used the analogy of a bucket of water that is lowered into a well to explain the resilience of the ego and the mind. He explained, *"In the bucket is water (the mind) which is merged with the well (Self), but the rope and the bucket (ego) still exist to pull it out again."*

Even after you have recognized the Self, the ego and mind still retain the strength to pull you away from this initial recognition. Through the consistent use of Self-inquiry, the mind will become established in the Self – the supreme state of Enlightenment. Ramana explained, *"In the case of Ganani (Enlightened Master) the rise or existence of the ego is only apparent and he enjoys his unbroken transcendental experience in spite of such apparent rise or existence of the ego, keeping his attention always on the Source. This ego is harmless; it is like the skeleton of a burnt rope – though it has a form, it is of no use to tie anything with."* Once the sacred fire of Self-inquiry consumes the ego and mind, they are like the *burnt rope;* they no longer have the power to pull you out of your natural state of being-consciousness-bliss. This is absolute freedom – the unwavering absorption in the Self.

Realization of the Self does not mean that you have to withdraw from the world. It is possible to recognize the Self and continue living a normal life. Once you have realized the Self, you are always aware of its infinite presence. The more you choose to not touch any thought, the more you will reflect the eternal depth, beauty, and grace of the Self. You might ask: "How does one remain absorbed in the Self?" This question comes from a sense of separation. Absorption in the Self is the unwavering recognition that you are That, the constant unchanging eternal Self! Focus your entire mind on That and you will know without a doubt that you are freedom itself. Once you have had a glimpse into the infinite nature of the Self, you will naturally become more aware of what thoughts you are *choosing* to identify with. If you continue to choose your thoughts over the Self – even more simply, if you practice desire on any level – you will continue to suffer.

Intellectual understanding is not enough to awaken to the Truth of Being. Remember, the *essential question* (Who am I?) is not merely an intellectual exercise. Any answer the mind can give *is not the answer.* Let me repeat this: *Any answer the mind can give is not the answer.* There is a mystical quality to Self-inquiry that provides a transmission of pure silent Grace, which transcends all intellectual knowledge. Through this transmission you see clearly to the source beyond any *intellectual* concept of what you *think* it is. The Self transcends everything known and unknown. You simply cannot think your way to enlightenment!

Once a person asked Ramana, *"Doesn't the inquiry "Who am I?" turn out in the end to be an empty formula? Or am I to put the question to myself endlessly, repeating it like an incantation?* Ramana replied, *"Self-inquiry is certainly not an empty formula; it is more than the repetition of an incantation. If it were mere mental questioning, it would not be of much value. Its very purpose is to focus the entire mind at its source. It is not, therefore, a case of one 'I' searching for another. Still less is it an empty formula, for it involves intense activity of the entire mind to keep it steadily poised in the pure Self-awareness. Self-inquiry is the one infallible means, the only direct one, to realize the unconditioned, absolute Being that you really are."*

Self-inquiry is the heart of Ramana's teaching. It contains the mystical Grace of divine love, which has the power to turn the tremendous force of the ego and mind toward the source – the Self.

Ramana often used the term *meditation* to describe Self-inquiry. Meditation from the perspective of Self-inquiry means to sit concentrating on your heart while at the same time asking yourself "Who am I?" Ramana insisted that Self-inquiry must be kept up until the very end – regardless of what visions, powers, or perceptions come. There is always the question *"To whom did they come?"* until only the Self remains. Through consistent use of Self-inquiry, your mind will become established in the heart, remaining absorbed in the Self even when you are busy with outer activity.

Your singular focus on the desire for freedom will lead you deep into the infinite depths of your own heart. Self-inquiry is a Holy Communion; it is transcendent of all knowledge. Through Self-inquiry, a natural stopping occurs. Once you stop, then freedom simply reveals itself, period. How this will show up for you cannot be planned. Initially, you might experience it as a deep unstoppable sadness, or a falling into an abyss, or you might start laughing uncontrollably. Its mysterious Grace can be bestowed upon you in a dream. It is beyond the realm of the mind. Whatever is needed to help you stop will occur when and where it is needed; you simply cannot know how it will show up for you.

The *essential shift* will occur of its own volition. In that moment, you will recognize something that cannot be recognized by the mind. Truth can reveal itself only when you stop and see the seer. A word of caution here: This inversion of mind that occurs does not represent the end ("I got it"). This glimpse into the infinite nature of the Self is only the beginning of a journey that has no beginning or end; it is eternally deep.

How your awakening will unfold for you will be exactly what is needed for you. All that is required is your singular desire for freedom. Then you will be open to receive the pure transmission of Grace that Self-inquiry represents. Let me repeat this: *How this recognition will occur cannot be planned. There is no strategy, method, or intellectual knowledge that will open the eyes of your heart.* Truth will simply reveal itself to you the moment it reveals itself. There is no telling when, or where, or how this will occur. The recognition of the Self is truly a Holy Communion which transcends all intellectual knowledge.

Once you have glimpsed into the infinite nature of the Self, your mind will attempt to own this as an experience. Freedom simply asks that you not return to following any thought, image, or feeling that emerges in your mind. Instead, remain aware of who you really are, the infinite Self. If you choose to follow your thoughts outward, you will suffer. Even after the *essential shift,* your mind can still be very tricky and can trap you into re-identifying with the thoughts, feelings, and images that emerge into your mind. Freedom requires that you simply remain vigilant toward what is eternally free from all thoughts, feelings, and emotions. Vigilance is a life-long process. As Papaji once said, *"You must remain vigilant to your very last breath!"* If there were any practice associated with freedom it would be the never-ending practice of vigilance. You might be wondering, "What is vigilance, and why is it so important?"

Vigilance

What is known as the "glimpse" into the silent, infinite presence within you happens in a fraction of a second. You cannot plan when this recognition of the Self will occur. It will happen when it happens; there is no strategy, formula, or method to realize the Self. Intellectual understanding alone does not take you into the truth of *Being*. Many find this difficult to understand. There is the idea that one must practice, and the question arises: "Is Self-inquiry a practice?" This is where things start to get a little tricky. Anything (even Self-inquiry) used as a strategy for getting something, reinforces the idea of a *doer* and objectifies freedom. The idea is, "If freedom is not here it must be somewhere else and I must *do* something to find it." This idea can actually render Self-inquiry ineffective. When Self-inquiry is used as a strategy, it transforms into a kind of empty questioning that will lead you in circles.

Once you awaken to the Self, vigilance plays an important role in remaining aware. Vigilance means remaining alert, aware of the thoughts, feelings, and words that can cause you to return to identifying with your story. Freedom demands that you remain vigilant until your very last breath. At its core, vigilance is surrender, and surrender is meeting death. Surrender and vigilance are the alpha and omega of Self-inquiry, the beginning and the end; there is no separation of the two. There is a danger that once you have the glimpse, the mind will try to own your experience of That or the idea, "I've got it. Now I am enlightened." The glimpse is then transformed into an inflated egoic idea of the Self. This inflation can last a lifetime or it can revert to a deflated ego ("I had it, but then I lost it.")

Absence of Doubt   *Vigilance*

Vigilance means keeping the mind humble when the inflated or deflated ego is present, which will enable you to recognize that neither inflation nor deflation is real. It is the recognition that the silence always remains whether "you got it" or "you lost it." Ultimately, vigilance means recognizing that you cannot get it or lose it, because it is always here, the eternal silence of the Self. It is who you really are, beyond the egoic *idea* of who you are. Ultimately, vigilance is the recognition that your story is not real.

Once you awaken to the Self, the mind and ego work harder to maintain your story. It is very easy to fall into various traps of the inflated or deflated ego. The simplest thing to remember is that *you are none of it.* You even have to throw out the idea, "I am the Self," or your mind might try to hold onto it as a concept, transforming it into a shadow of the Truth instead of the Truth itself. The mind can take anything and turn it into another aspect of the story of you. The key to vigilance is to keep the mind humble by not believing it for even a moment. Do not believe anything you think, period!

Enlightenment at its core is the recognition that you are freedom itself. It is the undeniable truth that you always were, you always have been, and you always will be the infinite silence of the Self. Surrender and vigilance work hand in hand to open your mind to the Truth of being, while Self-inquiry leads directly to the infinite depths of the ocean of the Self. When you look to see That which cannot be seen with the physical eyes, you are transported to the very core of your being. It is at this point that you might be wondering, "Where does this journey into the infinite Self take you?"

The Heart

Ramana said, *"When the mind, turning inward, inquires, "Who am I?" and reaches the heart, that which is 'I' (the ego) sinks crestfallen, and the One (Self) appears of its own accord as 'I-I.' Though it appears thus, it is not the ego; it is the Whole. It is the real Self."* Ego, mind, time, belief, desire, attachment, fear, and doubt all emerge from the I-thought. When you inquire into the source of the I-thought, your mind will fall naturally into the very core of your being, the sacred heart. As you enter the cave of your own heart, all that you thought you were will vanish. In the infinite silence of the heart, you will recognize that there is no ego, mind, time, belief, desire, attachment, fear, or doubt. You will know that there is no *doer* and no *doubter.* You will know without a doubt that you are freedom itself. You will recognize that you are silence supreme, a Holy Communion with the totality of the universe. You will be love falling in love with love, pure radiant *Being*; there will be no separation. It is the deep, undeniable recognition that who you really are is the purest, unimaginable, silent love. It is in this silence that you will see That which can only be seen with the eyes of the heart. You will see the seer.

Self-inquiry is not a concept or empty questioning. Self-inquiry is alive; it is a transmission of Grace that cannot be planned. No strategy, method, or practice can generate this radiant transmission. It is Truth revealing itself. As Jesus said, *"Know the Truth and the Truth shall set you free."* Remember, there is no doing. When you stop everything, when you are still and quiet, your mind will turn automatically toward the source. In that unknowable moment, a transmission of pure Grace will open your heart to the infinite unknowable depths of the eternal *One*, the

Alpha and the Omega, the beginning and the end. You will realize that you were never separate from That, the eternal presence of the Self; you only *thought* you were.

In every moment there is silence. Even in activity there is silence. Ultimately, silence is at the core of everything known and unknown. As Buddha's *heart* sutra reveals, *"Form is emptiness and emptiness is form."* At the very core of anything there is only silence.

Jesus said, *"Enter by the narrow gate; for the gate is wide, and the way is broad that leads to destruction, and many are those who enter by it. For the gate is small, and the way is narrow that leads to life, and few are those who find it."* Self-inquiry points to this very narrow gate revealing the way to freedom. To enter by the narrow gate, you must be willing to meet your own death, leaving everything you know behind. Even one thought is too much to carry through this gate! The heart is the gate; by being still, you will pass through it. The awakened heart of *Being* is the greatest of all gifts. As Jesus says, *"Where your treasure is will your heart be also."*

You have been given the opportunity to fall into the depths of your sacred heart through Self-inquiry, surrender, and vigilance. There is no end to the eternal depths of this inquiry. It will lead you into the core of your being, where you will discover for yourself the ancient gift of true faith, the complete and total *absence of doubt*. The moment you recognize the Self, you will be absolutely certain that this is true. In the heart, and only in the heart, you will discover the source of all thought. When you place your awareness into the infinite depth of the Self, it is there that you will recognize that there is no *doubter*, there is no *doer*, there is no-thing. Your heart is the sacred doorway that leads to a peace that surpasses all understanding. It is there that you will recognize a love so profound, so pure, that there are no words to fully describe it. The moment you surrender into the infinite pure conscious love of the Self, you will recognize in that eternal moment that you are the Cosmos.

You have had the opportunity to see that each of these aspects of the *essential context* can be either a gateway or barrier to freedom. This book has revealed that every aspect of the *essential context* – ego, mind, belief, time, desire, attachment, fear, and doubt – all emerged from the primal I-thought. You have had the opportunity to see for yourself that the *essential question* has the power to unlock the gateway of your own heart. The moment your enter your sacred heart, the core of your being, you will recognize that barriers or gateways are simply qualities of mind. The ultimate Truth lives only in the heart, where there are no gateways and there are no barriers to freedom. You are freedom itself!

How can there be a barrier or a gateway to what you already are?

No thought can contain the infinite Self. Even the *essential context* this book attempts to define does not represent a method for recognizing the Truth. There is no *doing* involved in this recognition. This does not mean that it does not require effort. Let me repeat: *This does not mean that it does not require effort.* To follow the path of Self-inquiry requires a great deal of effort. Self-inquiry is the most direct path to Self-realization, but it is also the steepest climb. It requires that you consistently focus your entire mind at its source, using Self-inquiry. No one can do it for you. There were people who wondered if Ramana's Grace alone were sufficient for Self-realization or if effort were required. Ramana's response to this was, *"If the guru could just give Realization, there would not be even a cow left unrealized."* There are many *perceived* barriers on the path to freedom. The Bhagavad Gita illuminates, *"Among thousands, perhaps one strives for Realization; among thousands who strive for Realization, perhaps one knows me as I am."* Jesus explains further, *"Many are called but few are chosen."* This is the paradox, there is <u>no</u> *doing,* yet intense *effort* is necessary for Self-Realization.

Ultimately, the belief that there is a barrier or a gateway to freedom is the final barrier. This is the final teaching of this book: There are no barriers to freedom; there are no gateways to freedom. You are already eternally free, but you *thought* you were not free. You believed in your thoughts, sensations, and feelings and became lost in the story of you. Self-inquiry simply leads your awareness to That which is free from it all – the Heart of Being.

Stop everything in this moment and listen to the silent breath flowing into in out of your lungs. This is the breath of life. What comes before your breath? There was a time when you were the entire ocean; then you became a wave. The moment you thought you were a wave, you forgot that you are the ocean. Who you think you are lives only in the world of the mind, the world of paradox, which is an endless house of mirrors. Let go of all of this. Even throw out this book! Let me say that again: *Throw out this book!* Or give it to someone else who is seeking freedom. Please do not allow anything (and I mean *anything*) to become a method for achieving enlightenment. Once you allow yourself to think you know *the way*, the narrow path of freedom is transformed into a *concept*, which is the dead past. In truth, *the way* does not exist; you already are where you thought you were going. The Truth is within you, not somewhere else!

The only purpose of this book is to point you to the Truth that cannot be expressed by any word or words. In an effort to ensure that this book provides the utmost clarity, I had a one-on-one conversation with Gangaji to discuss the *essential context*. This conversation provides a deeper look into the meaning of the *essential context*. How does Gangaji describe the *essential context?* Let's take a look at what Gangaji, a great teacher and master of Self-inquiry, has to say about it. I humbly offer this conversation to your open, innocent heart. May it open your heart to the Truth of *Being*.

Gangaji

A Conversation with Gangaji

Jill: The Essential Context is made up of definitions for ego, mind, time, desires, concepts, perception, and then finally, doubt. The ultimate truth is that these are neither barriers nor gateways. Most people see these as barriers to freedom, but the paradox is that they can be gateways, because if you have ego, then you have desire, and the desire for freedom is what sets you free, initially. So it's a double-edged sword, with of all of these.

Gangaji: That's right.

Jill: So what I'd like to do is go through each one of these and just get your feeling or what you think each one of these means, so that we can get to a core definition of what this means in the context of this lineage and this teaching that Ramana is relaying and transmitting.

Gangaji: I have to say that if you were interviewing Ramana, he might say it a little differently from me, and Papaji also might say it differently. So I can't say I know exactly what either one them might say. That's the beauty of this lineage: It cuts you free. Someone started interviewing me in Europe and said, "I want to ask you about the nature of ego. I suppose you would say ego doesn't exist," **coming from what he knew about the lineage and Advaita Vedanta. And I said "I wouldn't say that at all!" So it's like that. I can speak for myself, but I can't say that when we are talking about definitions, that I can speak for the lineage.**

That is fine. This is exactly what I wanted to get to, how *you* would respond. I recognize that you're not Ramana, you're not Papaji.

Gangaji: And I'm not speaking for them.

And I have some quotes from them, but let's start with ego, because when you look at spiritual communities, the biggest thing is ego. The goal of spiritual practice, for most people, is "how can I get rid of ego?" From a definition perspective, Ramana did say that Ego is the I-thought. And at one point you said that ego is the belief "I am the body." When you are speaking of ego, if it were the first time you were speaking or if it were to someone who has been following you for some time; what is ego?

Gangaji: What I would say, in this moment, is that ego is the *story* of you. So there's a physical aspect to it, which is the sensation of you as a body. And an emotional aspect to that, which is the feeling states that arise which you identify as "me." And the verbal, mental story that goes along with the history and the hopes and the desires. So you know, it's a big story.

Jill: And it started when you were a baby.

Gangaji: That's right. Or it's part of the human evolution. So it's programmed to start. The sense of 'me' as separate comes in, when, I don't know. I don't know that much about child development, but there's a time when you're two or one and a half, or three, where the sense of "me" as a separate individual arises, rather than "me" as everything I'm witnessing. And so that's ego, I would say.

Jill: There's also the aspect of ego, which you touched on, which is conditioning, and it's also the five senses, so "I *feel* separate."

Gangaji: You sense yourself as separate, because the body is separate from other bodies. *Apparently.* I mean, we can see scientifically now that even *that* is so fluid that you can't really say it's separate, but the experience is one of separation because of nerve endings and things like that.

Jill: Right. One of the biggest things that I deal with when I'm talking to people is that questioning, "But I don't know what you're saying because I feel different from you; I have a different body. I can leave the room and you're still there." You know, the whole dialog that emerges from that. And then there's the whole context of, "Well, the ego is bad, and if I'm going to be real spiritual I've got to get rid of it."

Gangaji: But that's the ego right there.

Jill: Right.

Gangaji: "I've got to get rid of it" is an egoic statement. That's about the story of "me" getting rid of ego. So what ego does, naturally, is separate itself from *other*, as some kind of survival evolutionary mechanism of the body/mind. And so then when a spiritual desire arises to be *free*, and one hears that to be free of the ego, then the ego takes that and goes, "Oh, I will be free. That will be my story then. It will be a spiritual story. So all I need is to get rid of ego." It then separates itself from so-called ego. And that's the mess! That's the confusion in almost every spiritual group I see, because the conditioning is so profound, so deep.

Jill: And in the community I came from, it was even taking the coconut to the monkey god, Hanuman, to have it cracked open to realize the nectar of the Self. But it was this, almost a ritual of exactly what we're talking about, trying to get rid of it, which is ego

179

itself. Even the taking of the little coconut off to the guru, which was a common gift.

Gangaji: It's like this *edge*, because you read what people say and they say you have to be rid of ego to wake up, but it just seems like since it is so hard to speak it and that's what your book is trying to do, and that's why I so fully support it. The challenge is to really speak as much as you can *around* it and then to recognize that whatever is being heard is most likely being heard through the filters of "my story," the ego. "What will I get from this?"

Jill: "How will I get enlightened?"

Gangaji: "How will I get something from this *for this story*?" So that in itself makes the understanding already polluted. So for the pure understanding of it, what's meant in surrendering to the guru, or to Hanuman is "Let me give you my story," that's what you have. And it *is* a coconut!

Jill: The coconut is supposed to be the knot of the ego, you crack it open and there's the nectar.

Gangaji: That's right! There's the nectar inside, so even *that* you surrender, so that

the ego doesn't take *that* as its own and enjoy the nectar.

Jill: Oh, that's right!

Gangaji: The saying is "pass the fruits on." The tendency is whatever the depth of the experience and truth of the depth of the experience is for the story to arise, out of the past habit of arising, and claim that for its own and make that another event in one's life, so enlightenment or realization becomes an event that happened to "me."

Jill: Right. And then people start to associate it with the spiritual experiences that they have, and then they go for more and more, which is what I was trapped in.

Gangaji: Oh, I think everybody that I know falls into that trap.

Jill: I knew there was something there, that the experiences were important.

Gangaji: It was a real taste and the experiences revealed that, and so naturally you want more. But it doesn't work.

Jill: No. And that's what led me to say that prayer for help, because I all of a sudden realized "What is this all about?" I went from satsang to satsang, to chanting, to whatever it was, from different teachers, and still there was a missing piece. And when I met you, in the stopping, that piece was revealed.

Gangaji: That's what I feel is the gift of this lineage, really. It's that somehow the search can stop. That's how Papaji phrased it, that the search can stop, and the attention can be turned back to who is it who is searching. So then the mind is turned back to the source of its story and there's no individual separate from anything there.

Jill: Right. The story just naturally falls away.

Gangaji: Yes. And then if it reappears, it's a transparent story, it's a movement of *dance*; you know, it's *movement* of energy – physical, emotional, or mental.

Jill: Right. Yes. It's amazing. It's totally amazing. I knew immediately. I mean, there was no doubt.

Gangaji: That's such good luck. Because then you don't have to fight with it. That's the ripeness.

Jill: I was really ready. It hit me on the head, boink!

Gangaji: You were ready. That's it. That's so good!

Jill: When you've gone from many different experiences and you finally get worn out. I was worn out.

Gangaji: Yes there's a disillusionment, or a worn-outness, that's really necessary. Otherwise you're still hoping for an experience that will give something to you, but you've seen through that to some degree, so it's like: There's something I'm not seeing.

Jill: Right.

Gangaji: And that's the humility, and the disillusionment, that mysteriously reveals some opening. And then you can't be denied. Then whatever it is you pray for is given.

Jill: And you stop in the prayer, too.

Gangaji: Yes!

Because you have to stop to go, "Wait a minute!"

Gangaji: Yes. That's right. That's right.

It was incredible, unforgettable. It was Grace, undeserved Grace.

Gangaji: Yes. How can anyone deserve all that is given?

Jill: So there's ego and there's also mind. So when you're speaking to mind, Ramana says, "Mind is nothing but the thought 'I.' Apart from thoughts there is no such thing as mind." And in <u>The Truth Is</u>, Papaji says, "Mind means past. When mind works it does not stay in the present, but digs the graveyard of the past."

Gangaji: So I would say that both of those quotes are referring to story. The story. And with Ramana, he's talking about that the story can't even go anywhere without this I-thought. That's the beginning of it. Then of course Papaji is elaborating on that: The story is not a story without a past. So the way I think of mind now though, is I would say is; there's a subconscious story that's operating and there's a conscious story that's operating. I would include, besides the I-*thought,* it's the I-sensation, and it's the emotional body. And I don't mean to separate those out; I think they're all intertwined. But because of Western psychology, and since

both **Papaji** and **Ramana** really weren't concerned with psychology at all, they don't have that understanding. So I think what the West has, that is really incredibly valuable, is the understanding of mind/body as this continuum of sensations and feelings and thoughts, or we could say I-sensations and I-feelings and I-thoughts.

Jill: I've often looked at the mind, because the mind emerges from Source or Self, almost as a bridge between the physical body and the Cosmos.

Gangaji: Or a reflector or something…

Jill: A reflector or mirror or a lens. And the lens, for most, is focused outwards. And what happens in this lineage is that it suddenly inverts.

Gangaji: That's right.

Jill: And you see very clearly to the Source, not some idea of it.

Gangaji: That's right. Because in the focus outward there is a pre-supposition of a *somebody* who is focused outward. So when the lens is reflecting back, you can't find "a somebody." It's not there. That's

the beauty of it; it's just a simple shift of turning and questioning what's been assumed; this I-thought, this I-body.

Jill: Right, and it's instantaneous.

Gangaji: Yes.

Jill: It's not like you have to sit there for hours and meditate.

Gangaji: That's right. It's not in time, because time is part of the story.

Jill: And it's unknowable when that inversion will happen. When I first met you, I thought I knew exactly what you were speaking. That's part of the reason this book evolved; because I came in with a set of information or ideas of what I thought these things meant, and what was required to transcend them. So I heard you and it was oh, yes, yes, yes! And I was having profound experiences with you as well, and then, all of a sudden, it just inverted and then, whoa!

Gangaji: That's the mystery. That's the mystery. You know, I think that's always a surprise – for the teacher, the student, everybody. Because you just can't tell who… I mean, I can't. Can you?

Jill: No! Because the people I think are hearing me, aren't.

Gangaji: And the people who look like they are…

Jill: I mean, I have some people who show up, who I think, "There's no way they're going to hear this," and then all of a sudden…

Gangaji: It's thrilling that way, because it's out of the realm of knowing. It is a mystery.

Jill: Right, right! Like the falling into the heart, almost like falling off a cliff. It just happens so quick. Unexpectedly. It can't be planned.

Gangaji: Yes.

Jill: Most spiritual communities are about planning, "How am I going to get there?"

Gangaji: That's right.

Or the strategy of getting close to the guru; or how long can I chant this chant; or how often can I chant this chant; or how often can I meditate? And these become these really advanced, in some cases, strategies.

Gangaji: Advanced stories. And powers are in that. There are siddhis that can be developed, there are yogas that can be learned, that actually refine the mind and the body so that it has great powers. But that's not it.

Jill: Right. And most people have this *ideal* of enlightenment. Enlightenment itself can stop someone, because they think, "If I become enlightened, then my life will be perfect."

Gangaji: That's "my life, my story."

Jill: Or they hold it up to the ideal of, you know, Jesus, which was definitely a big ideal for me – or Buddha. And if I have the life that *they* had my life would be beautiful.

Gangaji: And I will do what they did.

Jill: And I'll *be* like them! It's strange to watch, I mean, I did it myself.

Gangaji: Yes, me too.

Jill: The pretending of oh, 'if I'm really still and quiet…"

Gangaji: Holy. I'll *do* quiet. Or I'll *do* holiness, or I'll *do* being a saddhu. Rather than just being who you are.

Jill: Right. There's a kind of a relaxing, then a natural falling away occurs.

Gangaji: That's right. I think that's the key, Jill – *a natural falling away*. Because as long as there is someone doing it to get something, this is what has to be surrendered. There has to be a trust - that in the arising of the desire itself there is already the call home. And so whatever needs to be gone through will be gone through: all your experience-seeking, all your experiences, all your insights, and then the point where something unknowable, some shift occurs.

Jill: And it happens…

Gangaji: Just like that

Jill: Yes. Very quick.

And then there's Time, because the other mantra in spiritual communities is "staying in the moment." Especially now, you know the book *The Power of Now* came out and so this is the new thing, "I've got to get rid of my ego; I've got to stop my mind through meditation practices." That's how people think that's how they're going to *do* it. And then there's this issue of time; staying in the present moment.

Gangaji: Because that's the separation of you and the moment.

Jill: Right. You can't *stay* in the moment.

Gangaji: Exactly.

Jill: How are you going to do that? Because the moment is the moment.

Gangaji: It's here! And there's no way you cannot *be* in the moment. And so I think what happens is that when people daydream or space out, they think that's not in the moment. And so what gets called the moment is the awareness of the physical, emotional or mental plane that is happening right now. It's like a zen training or something, you know. That's what the moment is. But the moment is the Cosmos past, present and future, happening right now.

Jill: And as Papaji says, and even Ramana; ultimately there is even no present, or even any moment, because those are all concepts.

Gangaji: Those are all concepts, and they have to do with the story.

Jill: Right. So all three of those core things alone, without talking about anything else, these three things, I've seen, keep people trapped.

Gangaji: I do, too. Really, the concepts were initiated to point to that you are the moment.

Jill: The Truth.

Gangaji: But it gets heard, "Oh, I've got to work to be in the moment." But you are the silence. Someone said in this last retreat, "I'm 51% silent." It makes me never want to speak again, but you know, that's it – that's the challenge.

Jill: Because people get tangled up in the words. So I'm attempting here to try to untangle this.

Gangaji: I love it. I think it's a great challenge, a great attempt.

Jill: So then there's Desire, and people in spiritual community, they want to suppress desire, or if you're not in spiritual community, it's all about getting.

Gangaji: Acting out the desire.

Jill: Especially in this world, in the United States, it's about more, more, more, which is what I was caught in prior meeting you.

Gangaji: Right, so you're just figuring if I just get more of that, I'll get enough.

Right. And it's the core of suffering. There was one tape I listened to of you where you said, "When you practice desire, you suffer."

Gangaji: Yes.

And that's so true, because there's so much *doing* in it, and it definitely takes you out of the moment.

Gangaji: And your attention is on what you don't have.

Jill: Right. So it's somewhere else.

Gangaji: Your attention is somewhere and it's on what you don't have. It's on the evaluation of what you have versus what you don't have, and it's the "I" story. Papaji said, "The body is a desire body." Because the body story is a story about "I got to have enough food, I got to have enough shelter, enough protection, whatever." It's a desire body. And the

emotions and the thoughts are just fueled by that. And that just translates, when someone picks up the spiritual search, they just move those desires over to the spiritual thing. Whether it's renunciation of the body or acting out of the desires, it's the same thing. So the secret is to see the emptiness of desires or the transparency of them, and that, to me, is best revealed in the burning of them. So *not* repressing desires spiritually and *not* acting out desire, worldly, but actually recognizing this impulse for more; to get, and not moving. Just burning in it, but *not* moving.

Jill: Which becomes suppression.

Gangaji: Exactly. So burning is all I know to say about it, really. Because it *is* a fire, it's a huge fire. That's why people get so high when they fast, because they don't eat, and besides what biochemical stuff is happening, they don't eat, and they *want* to eat. And so there's this purification fire that happens, like whoa! They didn't act out on the desire, and there was fulfillment there. So desire is, I'd say, it's the biggest enemy portal. Was that the word you used? Gateway?

Jill: Gateway.

Gangaji: That's down to the crux of it. It seems to me that's the whole point of the I-thought even arising is for the desire for this body to exist, to continue to exist and to somehow procreate, whether it's procreation physically or procreation of ideas, like we're doing. It's this desire to share, you know, we've experienced something now that is so unbelievable, and we have this overwhelming, unstoppable desire to share it. So that's beautiful, you know. Of course there are traps in it.

Jill: Yes. Well, I've brought many people to you, because this is incredible!

Gangaji: Yes. It's just natural. You just *have* to. So we aren't physically procreating the DNA. But it's now in the realm of, we've discovered truth, and we want to share that, with the species, other bodies, with other aspects of ourselves. So desire is both a beauty and a horror.

Jill: Right. That's also one of the things I wanted to ask you, because it also is a double-edged sword. Because it can be a barrier or it can be the gateway.

Gangaji: Absolutely. It's *usually* the barrier, and it can be the gateway, because it is such a fire.

Jill: And that's what Papaji says is the desire for freedom. And with the desire for freedom you won't suffer.

Gangaji: That's right, because that desire for freedom consummates all the other desires. All the other desires are coming to tempt you away from that, but if your desire for freedom is really strong you're like the Buddha sitting with Maya coming, attacking.

Jill: And these things are just bouncing off you.

Gangaji: Yes

Jill: Very interesting.

I think these two are connected: desire and attachment. Also, I've seen in spiritual community is that one of the things people do to be more spiritual is to get rid of everything that they own.

Gangaji: Uh-huh.

Jill: They just give it away, they sell it, to be more spiritual and to have non-attachment as their goal. And of course over time they end up bringing these things back to them, but there's this point of, "I've got to give everything away to be more spiritual." But I feel like desire and attachment go hand in hand.

Gangaji: Yes, I think they do. There is kind of a different *tone* to attachment. You know, because it can feel very wonderful to give up everything! Because all of a sudden what we're attached to and what we desire, we are carrying, and it has weight; we give it up, and there's a freedom. It's like the guy fasting or whatever, you know, whoa! So there's this freedom but the attachment is actually more subtle; it's an attachment to that state of freedom which resulted in the giving up attachments. So it's like the attachment comes back before the stuff comes back.

Jill: Right.

Gangaji: Because then, by the time the stuff starts coming back there's kind of a disillusionment with this, you know, giving this stuff up, because I lost my state...

Jill: Right! Because it didn't last.

Gangaji: The state of exultation in giving it up. And so that's actually good because you see it's not about the stuff, it's recognizing the natural biological attachment of the body/mind to the emotional mind and the mental mind to the body/mind and emotional mind, that they are attached, those three minds – those three aspects of mind, are attached, and seeing through that, that there is a *seeingness*, a pure seeingness that's already unattached to all of it. And yet, it has no problem with the attachment of it, no problem with the body acting out its desire for food, or the emotions, you know, wanting love, or the mind wanting to be able to speak what can't be spoken. Then it is quite beautiful, the play of leela. It just seems like it turns into that same poison of desire when this life force energy is given to keeping attachments and getting more attachment.

Jill: Holding on to what I have.

Gangaji: *Or* the attachment of letting go – the flip side.

Jill: Right, the other side of it. Also hooked up to attachment or non-attachment is the idea, "If I live in poverty, you're holier or more spiritual."

Gangaji: Like Jesus, because that was a part of his teaching. His people were in poverty, you know. It's *fine* if people want to live in poverty. But I was just reading something about how Jesus really spoke to the people and did something very different from what had ever been done. He took it from the gods being up here and having these exalted things. His parables were really down to earth, just as you are, basically. He talked about sheep and mustard seeds. It had never been done before! And poverty was about that. They were living in a slave culture; they *were* in poverty, except the ones who were making money off the Romans and the synagogues. So there was a purity there that's so beautiful, that people *want.* But it usually gets corrupted. Not always. We just came from Assisi. St. Francis, you know, went into total poverty and was absolutely pure and beautiful; so it definitely can work. But once anything becomes *the* formula to give me what I want, it's already polluted.

Jill: Because there's already a thread of desire there.

Gangaji: That's right. It's about "me" still. It's not about God; it's not about true freedom; it's about me and what I want, so I'll give up everything to get what I want.

Jill: Francis of Assisi to me is an example of pure devotion, but he wasn't doing it to *get.*

Gangaji: That's right, that's the key. He wasn't polluted. Just like Ramana is not polluted, so you can feel that. And a lot of the Franciscans I saw were absolutely beautiful. I don't know what they're like, you know, when they're on their off hours, but they were radiating a kind of purity that I was really surprised and happy to see. Still very much in the church, of course, but beautiful; radiating beauty.

Jill: I've often felt that the reason the church and the religions that came up around Christ or Buddha or any of the great teachers, the reason it still works for people on some level is because there are those core truths that are there.

Gangaji: That's right. It's a mystical Truth, and those people in the religion

who realize that, those are the ones we love. Some of the saints and certain of the mystics, St. John of the Cross and St. Teresa. I mean, we have examples. They're there.

Jill: And there are some that I'm sure we don't know about.

Gangaji: That's right. Most of them we don't know about. Most of them we know nothing about.

Jill: And that's also a mystery.

When we talk about religion, there are beliefs and concepts that come out of truth. But these beliefs and these concepts can also delude the mind.

Gangaji: I'd say they *usually* do. I think you can end up back where you started with your belief, but you have to give up the belief, because if you're following your belief to get what it is you want, it's polluted.

Jill: Right.

Gangaji: Or the concept. So that's the thing about renunciation. It's to just give it all up, in a second, in a split second – to

have nothing, to have no enlightenment, to have no relationship with God, to have no saints. Just to have nothing and then, purity is there, it's already *here*. And then naturally your life takes a certain form, which may or may not be like the lives or the concepts you were following; but if it is like the concepts you were following, it's purified.

Jill: It's more natural.

Gangaji: That's right. It just naturally suits you.

Jill: Right. It would naturally occur versus, "I'm going to force it."

Gangaji: That's right; because this is what it "should" look like.

Jill: Right. "I'm going to *be* like Ramana." "I'm going to *be* quiet." That's a little different than what we're talking about because we're going deeper – beyond the belief.

Gangaji: That's right, because you're not going to be anything, quiet or not quiet.

Jill: And then there's the whole concept of, "Oh, I'm nothing."

Gangaji: Oh, boy!

Jill: And I've seen people do that, and you can't even do that. You have to not touch any of those thoughts that come.

Gangaji: Yes. Papaji would say, "Don't cling even to emptiness. Don't cling to anything, no thought. Don't let the mind touch a thought." And that's what you are. That *is* a moment, and that's always here. Everything else that's here is brought to that, and disappears.

Jill: Right. I see that happening, the beliefs, depending on people's backgrounds, whatever beliefs they might have, and it might just be religious or it might just be…

Gangaji: And it may be subconscious; they might not even know it.

Jill: Right. In fact, in the last satsang here in Marin with you, I had the experience of a subconscious thing all of a sudden just coming into my awareness, and then also being blown away.

Gangaji: That's great.

Jill: And that was the whole concept of how one should be as a minister or a spiritual teacher. But I didn't even know it was there.

Gangaji: Yes. That's the beauty. I love that; it's like, "Wow, that's *there*?" It's so surprising, because you haven't been operating from that.

Jill: No. But you see it.

Gangaji: It's the *natural* burning of vasanas then.

Jill: I saw it for a split second and then this concept kind of just blew apart; it's like an explosion.

Gangaji: That's great, isn't it? On fire.

Jill: But it was mysterious because it was not *known* to me; like you said, I wasn't acting from it.

Gangaji: It was subconscious.

Jill: And I think a lot of people have those things that they're not aware of.

Gangaji: Yes, that's probably 90%, and 10% is conscious. And it may even be deeper than subconscious. Maybe it's

built into the body, or past lives or threaded through into the cells. It's like the fixation: You're not even aware that it's operating, so even deeper than fixation there can be things operating that are so merged with the field that you don't recognize them until they just arise. And that's the beauty of just being in life, because you're in situations where whatever can arise will arise.

Jill: Right. So life itself becomes a satsang.

Gangaji: It is.

Jill: I've heard you say that before. Once you've been to satsang, then everything, every place you find yourself in is an opportunity to go deeper.

Gangaji: There's the mirror.

And to say, "Oh you know, this is really pushing my buttons." Why is that?

Gangaji: And my buttons shouldn't be pushed.

Jill: Oh yeah, they shouldn't be. It's, "Oh, I should be the good little girl."

Gangaji: "I should *never* be angry!"

Jill: That's another spiritual thing, "I'm going to be the good little girl or the good little boy…"

Gangaji: Oh yeah, that's a big one. That's Sunday School.

Jill: When the guru comes, everybody transforms into…

Gangaji: Yeah, they all look so good, I'm always so surprised to hear how everybody acts.

Jill: But you know, you witness this, especially if you go to a big ashram.

Gangaji: Oh yeah!

Jill: You see everybody working away. They're mad, they're doing all this stuff, and all of a sudden the guru walks in and they're just transformed.

Gangaji: Well part of that is the guru's grace; it does transform them. The other part is just really old, sibling rivalry; you want to be saved, so you're sweet so your mother loves you, so she feeds you, and if she's got thirteen kids, if you're the sweetest, best one, she's going to feed you

before she feeds that bad, horrible one. It's really primal stuff, animal stuff. You know, like birds.

Jill: It all comes back to the whole – everything we've been talking about – it's all so interconnected and that is what makes it tough, to separate it out.

Gangaji: You can separate it out temporarily and then you have to put it right back in, because if it's *held* separate, then it doesn't work. But it's just separating it, like a microscope, you know; okay, we'll focus on *that*, now. And just by focusing on that, we've lost *this* picture, so we go back.

Jill: And if you focus in too far then you've lost the *big* picture.

Then there is this whole concept of doubt, or this feeling of doubt. I know in my own experience, even though I was having profound experiences, I still had doubt. I would have the moments of awakening or moments of Grace, and then doubt would return. I want to read this quote, because this is one of the most profound things I've heard from Ramana:

"There is no use in removing doubts. If we clear one doubt, another rises, and there will be no end of doubts. All doubts will cease, only when the doubter and his source have been found. Seek the source of the doubter, and you will find he is really non-existent. Doubter ceasing, doubts will cease."

Gangaji: That's great. That's beautiful. It's like doubting the doubter. Everything is doubted but the doubter. What more can be said? That's so perfect.

Jill: It's *so* perfect. And I've pointed that to people who have doubt. A lot of people have doubt.

Gangaji: Oh, I had doubt. People make the mistake: They think doubt is questioning. And questioning is legitimate; one must question. But doubt is something else.

Jill: It's a skeptic.

Gangaji: Yeah. There's a cynicism or a skepticism or a denial; it's different from questioning. Questioning is open-ended and doubt is closed. I definitely had doubt; everybody I know has had doubt. There was a point though, with Papaji, where I had to recognize the doubts and just refuse to follow them. And almost in

that moment, they did arise some after that, but from that moment on they weren't *empowered* like they had been, because I'd been kind of believing that my doubts were like my proof that I'm really conscious or something. So without doubts, maybe I'm not conscious; maybe I'm totally brainwashed or something.

Jill: Oh, I see.

Gangaji: So, there was really trusting the doubting, more than trusting the realization. So there was a leap, another leap off a cliff, where there was a willingness: You know, if I'm really making a big mistake, so be it. I'm making this mistake then. I'm going to go all the way in this mistake, but I'm not going to listen to this voice: "You could be making a mistake."

Jill: Right. Which is the Skeptic.

Gangaji: That was a huge point. That was a kind of conscious recognizing it, and it was from a very old, deep, Christian conditioning that arose, about, "My God, I'm gonna go to hell, because I'm following this Hindu guy, of all things." I mean, maybe because it was so blatant that I could see that but it felt very real.

But there was a kind of courage in having to say, "I'm not going to follow it." It sounds like it's making sense, but I'm not going to follow it. There is something big happening here that I trust. It's like with a lover, or a new job or whatever, you can have all the mind stuff, but it's like, "Okay, I'm going for it anyway."

Jill: Right.

Gangaji: I'm doing it any way.

Jill: Something deeper is saying this is right?

Gangaji: No, it could be a mistake, so it's not like blindly, but consciously.

Jill: Would you say that the flip side of doubt is faith, when you're talking about courage?

Gangaji: Yes, I *like* faith, you know. Faith gets a bad rap in spiritual circles, and I've probably talked badly about it too, but there's a kind of faith that's really alive and open-ended, and it's based on an experience that is deeper maybe than the present moment experience, but it's still alive, even if you're not feeling it, or seeing it or thinking it, it's still alive and it generates the courage to say *no* to the

doubt. Or for the early martyrs to say, "Okay, eat me alive."

Jill: Or like Moses, if you go to the Bible. He had faith, and I'm sure he must have had doubts.

Gangaji: Yeah, he was a man.

Jill: He couldn't even speak very well, and he was supposed to go talk to this king. You can imagine what this guy was going through, but he went anyway. He had the courage to go.

Gangaji: Well that's it. In satsang, people will say, "I'm scared to death," but they're up there, speaking, in front of hundreds of people. So they're scared to death, they don't believe they can do it, but there's an indefinable power that can be surrendered to, consciously. Where the doubts may appear, but it's not even a question of following them. It's like, "Oh, that's a doubt."

Jill: The reason I chose the title *Absence of Doubt* to me was like the ultimate faith. If you are absent of doubt, you are certain.

Gangaji: You're certain then. So it's really certitude. There was this moment with Papaji, I would say from that moment on,

even though that wasn't my most profound realization, that wasn't the essential shift that happened, the doubt didn't have the power it had, so the certitude could *be* there. Before it couldn't be there because the doubt was like, I was too scattered.

Jill: It could have the power to take it away.

Gangaji: Yes. Certitude; I think, that's what everybody wants, and that's what's *available*. Because, what it is you want is truly what you are. If what you want is to be a holy person or a good person, or an always sweet person, that's another story.

Jill: Because that's an idea. That goes back to what I was saying earlier, about how people think once they're enlightened, it's going to be Shangri-La.

Gangaji: Oh, they think they're going to be totally *psychic*. They're going to know everything that's happening. They think all kinds of things.

Jill: It also is a concept.

So then I come to Self-inquiry, because Self-inquiry is the key to this lineage.

211

Gangaji: That's right.

Ramana talks about how it's not just a simple questioning. I've had people ask me what I'm doing, and I say that it's based in Ramana's teaching of Self-inquiry, and they say, "Oh! Self-inquiry." I guess it's a big thing in therapy, if you are a therapist.

Gangaji: Oh, really?

Jill: Or in that field if you say Self-inquiry, it means something else.

Gangaji: Aha, you mean looking at what you're feeling, what your truth is.

Jill: Self-inquiry from a therapist's perspective, when they're working with their client.

Gangaji: Aha, I hadn't thought of it like that. Very interesting; I didn't realize that. I should know that, speaking to people. I should know that because it could be so easily thought that that's what you're talking about.

Jill: Right. And so I've noticed this and…

Gangaji: So it's really inquiry into Self.

Jill: Not self-inquiry as a way for people to deal with their past wounds, you know.

Gangaji: That's right. It's discovery of Self. Investigation. Yeah, it's this word "Self," because it means ego and it means totality.

Jill: It means a lot of different things to different people.

Gangaji: So inquiry. It's so tricky!

Jill: God inquiry!

Gangaji: Psychology, of course, is dealing with ego, and so naturally what's talked about here, you could talk about it all along, with the ego.

Jill: Right. And they dismiss it because it's like, "Oh, I do it with my clients, so how's it going to help me?" It's just a subtle thing that I noticed. People don't even understand the core of this teaching, which is Self-inquiry. Which is not just questioning, which also can be come a thing: Who is it that's eating? Who is it that's sleeping?

Gangaji: Oh, yeah. Gosh.

Jill: It's as Ramana was saying here: "*The purpose of self inquiry is to focus the entire mind* [which in and of itself is hard to grasp] *on its source, and it reveals the truth that neither the ego nor the mind really exists, and enables one to realize the pure, undifferentiated being.*" He's so eloquent.

Gangaji: So beautiful, so pure, in that.

Jill: So it's that whole, *all* of it, focusing it in.

Gangaji: That's why I use the word *meeting*, or sometimes I talk about an embrace. In a real embrace, it is your whole being that's in this embrace; your mind, your body, and your feelings. And in that, there is no mind, body, and feelings. There's just this love, or the mystery of the meeting. You couldn't even call it *love*, because it gets even deeper than love; it's profound discovery.

Jill: Right. Because the words can keep you from hearing it.

Gangaji: With the words you stay mental.

Jill: Well love, to a lot of people, means sex.

Gangaji: Yeah. That's right. That's as much as most people know about, that's as deep as they've gotten. That's where

they've discovered surrender, or non-existence of self. So you start where they are. So it's *that*, but without the sexual stimulation or excitement. It's the quiet space, and you don't have to do something to get it. You don't need to generate the tension to get it. But that's of course why sex would be so good, you know, because if we're talking about this psychological counterpoint, in which ego is the imitation of "I," so of course sex would be the place where the absolute ultimate is experienced, so it can continue.

Jill: Right. And I can keep doing it to get that feeling.

Gangaji: It's brilliant. It's a brilliant putting it together.

Jill: Right. And then the Self-inquiry, *true* Self-inquiry goes beyond all concept. It has nothing to do with mind even, or any intellectual understanding. It's just really going to that source.

Gangaji: Yes. It's recognizing all is Self. So what is here, what is this? How is this Self? Who is this Self? Where is this Self?

Jill: Or as Jesus said, which is one of my favorite quotes from him, "Know the truth, and the *truth* shall set you free." He doesn't say *you* do anything.

Gangaji: Yes. Beautiful.

Jill: You could almost reinterpret that to mean, "Recognize Truth, and the Truth itself sets you free."

Gangaji: That's right. Truth *reveals* freedom. That's my favorite quote of his too. I love that. It's true. It's absolutely true.

Jill: That's one of those core truths that are in the Bible; those seeds, that can't be destroyed and have survived.

Gangaji: Survived religion.

Survived religion, and survived translation!

Gangaji: Yes. That's really, that's great.

Jill: You also have that translation layer and you know some of it has been lost. And I think he spoke the way he did to insure, to the best of his ability, that it wouldn't get changed.

Gangaji: Oh, he's so beautiful, speaking simply like that. He's so brilliant to be able to speak simply. I love this book for that; it's really out of this desire to speak it in a way that the mind can't translate it, that the ego can't translate it into its own language so that it penetrates through.

Jill: One of the things I've noticed since I've been with you is how powerful the mind and the ego are, and how subtle it gets.

Gangaji: Oh yes!

Jill: How important vigilance becomes, because it's so subtle.

Gangaji: But that's its beauty, you know. That's what makes it fun. It's the leela, leela fun.

Jill: Like Medusa coming to get you.

Gangaji: It is like Medusa.

Jill: Slithering, it's amazing to watch.

So, the other thing I wanted to speak to you about: The heart is the gateway to truth, or the gateway to the Self. People get confused by the physical heart versus the sacred heart.

Gangaji: But you know, somebody sent me a long fax about the *physical* heart, and it is an amazing organ. I haven't read the whole thing, but it's astounding. In Chinese medicine it was called the Supreme Emperor, because everything was geared to taking care of that. You know, your brain can go before your heart can go.

Jill: You can still live without your brain.

Gangaji: Yes, that's right. So when I ran into this problem about the heart and speaking about the heart, I changed it to the *core.* Sometimes I forget to say "core," and I say heart. But it's really the *core,* and the core is the Universe. So the core in everyone is the Universe that everyone is in. And it's that flip, you know, so if somehow you can just direct people to "What is in the core?" in you, in any particular emotion, especially the negative ones that arise, in any body that you see, in any thought, in the *core* is this emptiness that is not empty, but it's transparent space. Yes, that's it. To me then that *is* the Self. It's the way of the Self and the way to It-Self. Because it is the Self.

Jill: And Papaji talks about how this teaching has to land in your heart. If it lands in your mind, it's just dry.

Gangaji: It's a mess...

Jill: It's just dry understanding.

Gangaji: It's Corinthians, you know?

Jill: Really?

Gangaji: You know, "Though I speak of angels, though I have all the wisdoms, I'm just a clashing brass and tinkling cymbals, without love."

Jill: That's right! Corinthians, Chapter 13. Yes. Right.

Gangaji: So there it is. You can have all the wisdom of all the sages of all time. Without love, it's nothing. You missed it.

Jill: Because that is the key. If there's a key or a gateway, it's the heart.

Gangaji: It's the gateway to itself.

Jill: And Ramana talked about the only reason he used the heart in association with the body is because most people are still identified with themselves as a body, so there's the physical heart, but then he called it the sacred heart.

Gangaji: Right. Well, I think the physical heart, because most people actually do feel – you know you *feel* your heart break. When it breaks, you actually feel it in the place of your heart.

In your chest.

Gangaji: So there's some relationship there that's biological and emotional, and spiritual, because you can *enter* there. And that's the Christ, too, with the heart.

Jill: Right. He's always pointing to his heart. Almost all the paintings of Christ, they have the sacred heart, and he's pointing to his heart.

Gangaji: It's like, "This is the way".

"This is the way," right! And recently, because of this teaching, Holy Communion means so much more to me. Because Christ is speaking to a different consciousness, a very survival, poverty consciousness, as we were speaking of, and here he's trying to tell them, "This is my body. Merge with me." But not 'me' the man, which is how it got interpreted; but he's talking about merge with the Self, with God; You are That!

Gangaji: Yes. It's here, in even this piece of bread, or in this wine.

Jill: Right. And so ingesting it! How could you get any closer? They're eating this, they're drinking this.

Gangaji: It's inside you. It's beautiful, a holy communion.

I love that. Holy Communion, to me, especially as a small child, I always thought was so *odd*. That this is the body of…

Gangaji: It's weird, because they don't know how to talk about it. It's one of those things they say: "Don't ask."

Jill: Right, I can remember thinking, "Isn't this a little weird? I thought he rose again, I mean, how can we eat his body?" It was just strange.

Gangaji: It is a little strange, until you penetrate it, and then it's absolutely beautiful, and simple.

Jill: Right. Then you can see what he was really trying to say. He was trying to almost give them a demonstration of how close he was. That it wasn't separate in any way.

Gangaji: That's beautiful.

Jill: And that all ties into the heart, the sacred heart.

You speak of this teaching, not as a teaching but an invitation to stop, to be still and to be silent.

Gangaji: Yes.

And Papaji says that over and over again, in anything you read about him. And people miss that, too.

Gangaji: Oh boy, I know. They start *trying* to be still, and tell me how they were still most of the day, but not… And it's like, "Oh boy, I shouldn't have said it that way."

Jill: So the way I've been looking at this when I speak to people about this… The silence naturally happens when you stop and the stillness naturally happens. I tell people that sometimes you have to move to stop, so it's not about physically stopping your body or trying to control.

Gangaji: That's right. It has nothing to do with the physical, really.

Jill: But when your thoughts arise, the way I hear stopping, is to not follow those thoughts. To stop chasing those thoughts.

Gangaji: To not follow them *outward*. If you follow them inward, if you re-wind it, and Papaji used to do this with people a lot, and I did it early on, and I see Eli does it sometimes. If you actually follow a thought back to where it arose from.

Jill: I've seen you do this where you take a sentence and you make them go back.

Gangaji: You end up in silence, it's like, "Oh!" For an instant there is just the silence. We're so conditioned to follow outward, and then to build. So either to not follow outward or to follow the thought back to its source. To actually *use* the thought to go back to its source.

Jill: Right. You just reminded me of something that Jesus said: "It's not what comes into your mouth that can harm you, it's what comes *out* of your mouth."

Gangaji: Aha! That's great!

So that could be interpreted to be mind. Your mind focused outward can hurt you, but your mind focused inward takes you back to the Truth.

Gangaji: That's right. That's right. It takes you back.

Jill: So that's all. I bring him up only because…

Gangaji: Oh I love it, I love it. I'm a devotee.

Jill: There is such a beautiful presence with him.

Gangaji: What a being!

Jill: To me the crucifixion was the ultimate demonstration of "You are not your body." That's misinterpreted as well, but he was trying to show them. "I am not *this*, my word will go on."

Gangaji: And boy, didn't it!

Jill: Yeah. It's incredible

Gangaji: Pretty amazing, from really a small group of people.

And to go there, even with all the turmoil in Jerusalem, to *be* in Jerusalem and to go to these holy sites, and you know that he was there. There's an energy about it.

Gangaji: Yes. There absolutely must be.

Jill: Because people grow silent. They stop there. They think about it there.

Gangaji: That's right. It's like Ramana ashram, and Assisi, and Bhodgaya. Wherever it is that holy people have stood up and lived and given their lives to the Truth, the whole place is transformed then, forever. This is what our whole planet is calling for now from all of us. It's time, we have to discover this, live this, surrender to the mystery occurring.

Jill: Right. And it's challenging now. Especially some of the leaders in this country have… I hear them, and I understand where they're coming from, because I've been there myself, but I also know, from a broader perspective, a more enlightened perspective. It's painful, to see the suffering this is propagating.

Gangaji: Oh my goodness, it's primitive, you know, it's very primitive.

Jill: It's ancient.

Gangaji: This is like "an eye for an eye" kind of stuff.

Jill: It's shocking to me because there's an actual belief that somehow *this* time it's going to be different!

Gangaji: I know, it's humiliating, isn't it? Or humbling, let us say.

Jill: I mean, it's laughable, this has been happening for centuries.

Gangaji: This is the story. This is the collective story of the human animal.

Jill: It could be knights with armor, and it's the same story playing itself out again.

Gangaji: And before that, chimpanzees in the tree.

Right. And to be the observer of it, but to not spiritualize it to the point where you don't take action.

Gangaji: Yes, that's the whole thing. To just be real.

Jill: To be present.

Okay, so stopping, the stillness and the silence. Silence is the core of this teaching, but it's a natural thing.

Gangaji: That's right. It's not *getting* to silence; it's recognizing that silence is here. Silence is in every moment, *is* every moment, and everything else in that moment just appears, and disappears, takes form and loses form.

Jill: But it's still silence. I had the realization that it is impossible to leave silence. "How do you leave Silence?" You *can't.*

Gangaji: Because you are silence.

Jill: It's like saying how do you leave the Self, you can't. But the mind thinks it can.

Gangaji: Yeah, well that is the split. That's separating itself as one from another. Silence then becomes the other.

Jill: Or something to get. Or something to be, or to try to be.

Gangaji: Or to keep.

Jill: You ask people to tell the truth. And I see a tendency to tell relative truths.

Gangaji: Well I think that's where people start, and as a starting place that's okay. Maybe I should say, don't *stop* telling the truth. Because the truth may first be, "Oh, I'm angry." But most people will say, "I'm angry. I didn't know I was angry" and then go *lateral* with that.

Jill: Instead of…

Gangaji: Okay, you're angry. What else is true, what's under that? The relative truth is honesty, be honest with yourself, but the Truth is under it all, and so to get to the Truth, I think that the relative is usually necessary. Ramana when he had the fear of death, he was overcome with this fear, he didn't pretend he wasn't afraid you know, but what he did was lay down and experience the fear, and really inquire into the fear.

Jill: Right. He didn't run away. Meeting fear is telling the truth, and also seeing the story.

Gangaji: Yes. Because in telling the truth there's fear, and there's the possibility of meeting it and the possibility of telling some story which will help you avoid it, or deny it, or act it out in some way, so to tell the truth is to see, "Oh! there are all these options." *Truth* is not an option; it's there. But the mind has options of what to *do* with the Truth, and what people usually do is avoid it. Because it's uncontrollable; it's huge and it's vast. And so the stories get stacked on *top* of it. So telling the truth relatively just can penetrate through to a certain point. And then as you say, then it's the mystery, when that flip happens.

Jill: When that lens inverts.

I wanted to speak of three other things because I think they're important: meeting death, surrender (which we've touched on), and vigilance. Vigilance to me is interesting because people do have that moment, the glimpse, where their mind inverts. But then there's this idea or a concept that jumps in that says, "Now that I'm awake, I don't need vigilance."

Gangaji: That's the inflation. That's inflated ego, "Now my story is complete – I *got* it."

Jill: Right.

Gangaji: "Therefore, I don't need anything. And that inflation can last a lifetime; it does with some people, you know. Usually, though, it's followed by deflation, because certain events happen, or the person is actually honest enough that there's a recognition and there's a *loss* then, of "what I had." That's the inflation/deflation pendulum. But the vigilance is the recognizing that all of that's going on: I got it, I lost it, I got it, I lost it – While the silence is still here. It didn't have anything and it hasn't lost anything.

Jill: Right. It holds it all.

Gangaji: And it's conscious.

Jill: Right.

So the vigilance is, as Papaji said, "To your last breath". It's important because the ego gets more and more subtle. So it's about remaining aware.

Gangaji: It's remaining aware and the mind remaining humbled, because there's the recognition of "I am the Self," but very subtly the mind can take that over, and if there's a true vigilance there's a recognition when the mind takes that over, and it's like not buying into it. You can feel puffed up but you don't buy into it, you know, *"Oh, puffed up!"*

It doesn't carry you off.

Gangaji: It's not real; it's recognized to not be real.

Right. So I wanted to touch on vigilance and also surrender. I didn't understand surrender. I thought I did but, because of the spiritual communities I was in, I saw surrender like *bowing before*. But that was creating a sense of separation. So surrender was either bowing to, or giving up, like "I surrender" with my hands up. But I didn't get the *merging* quality of it.

Gangaji: Because it *really* means surrender. It really means surrender your story.

Jill: Right. Which is meeting death.

Gangaji: And it takes us back to the coconut, back to Hanuman. It's really surrender your coconut. It's meeting death, and it's horrifying so we'd much rather *do* surrender, which keeps us busy, than really take a moment and *be* surrender.

Jill: Yes. *Be* surrender, that's the key.

Gangaji: And then it's the same as vigilance. That's where they meet then.

Jill: And there's one final thing, and this is the thing that made my mind flip, and that was when Papaji, in the book, *The Truth Is*, said to "see the seer." And he said that when Ramana told him that, then everything stopped.

Gangaji: That's beautiful.

Jill: See the see-er, then that's the teaching.

Gangaji: That's it.

Jill: There was that mystical moment when it inverted, so that's a key piece.

Gangaji: Well, that's inquiry. So somehow it was said in a way, in that moment, where it could actually penetrate. Then the inquiry was alive in you.

Jill: It was beyond the *concept* of inquiry.

Gangaji: That's right. It had nothing to do with the concept then, because it was alive. There was a transmission in that. So the transmission, "see the seer," you *heard* that. You got that in that moment, so your mind turned to see the see-er.

That's inquiry, right there. That what's pointed to by the phrase.

Jill: Or the questions. The questions are trying to lead you to that.

Gangaji: Who can say how many people have been able to read that phrase and get it? Not everybody. That's the mystery, but some people have.

Jill: Oh, it was like someone went "Blink!" and I just stopped in that moment. That's when stopping actually happened. And I had the profound spiritual experiences with you, but in *that* moment.

Gangaji: That's   it.   That's   what's necessary. Well, I used to say I'm doing this, I'm hoeing the garden for Papaji, getting all the weeds out.

Jill: Creating a clear space.

Gangaji: So I'm very happy to hear that.

Jill: So a lightning bolt can come through.

Gangaji: And you're a lightning rod.

Jill: Right. Just one final thing, because this is something that I personally wanted to know.

Papaji, when he died, his last teaching was, "Where is the Buddha?" What does that mean to you? To me it means things, but what is the deeper teaching in that for you?

Gangaji: Well, when I heard it, I heard it from one of the people who were with him as he was dying. He was great; he was relating everything that happened in the last couple of days, and he related how different people came in and said different things. It's a koan, really. "Where is the Buddha?" is a koan. So really the only answer is silence.

Jill: Yes.

Gangaji: But it's not a dead silence of course.

Jill: It's not the word "silence."

Gangaji: No. It's the silence.

Jill: I went to his website and saw that and that made me stop. Because I knew he wasn't talking about the man Buddha. I was awake enough to know that.

Gangaji: Well, one of his Indian devotees thought he *was*; maybe he was having delusions, you know, from the drugs or

something. So everyone has a different take on it, you see? But to me what that says is really how are you using it, so for me everything Papaji says points me to inquiry. That's who Papaji is in my life. Whether he's deluded, whether he's raving because of the drugs they're giving him, that doesn't even matter, that's secondary. His life is a pointer to that; more than a pointer, it is the core of that. And so, there it is.

Jill: Right, it all returns to silence.

Gangaji: Yes. It's never separate from silence. Because even in the activity if you look in the core, investigate the core of any activity, there is silence. Silence then is activity, activity is silence. That's what the Buddha says, "Form is empty, emptiness is form."

Jill: Right. I sat with the Dalai Lama for four days and he went through the whole sutra.

Gangaji: Oh, that's great.

Jill: It was beautiful. It took four days to get to that one statement, "Form is emptiness and emptiness is form," and *that* is the teaching.

Gangaji: That's right. That's his teaching. Full circle. All is one.

Jill: And that's the heart sutra.

Gangaji: That is right! Of course! It's the heart sutra, what else could it be?

Jill: When I heard that, I didn't even know it. I sat there with the Dalai Lama but I never knew it was the heart sutra. I was just, you know, I'm there with the Dalai Lama, taking notes.

Gangaji: Trying to figure it out.

Jill: Going through the history, and all the different dynasties, I mean, he went through the *whole* thing. And so when Eli said, "Oh, that's the heart sutra," and it was like, well *that* makes sense.

Gangaji: Isn't it beautiful? It's all, East and West then, North and South there it is in the heart, in the core.

Jill: And all of it is silence.

"There is nothing covered that will not be revealed and hidden that will not be known."

- Jesus

Let there be Peace and Love among all Beings
of the Universe. Let there be Peace.
Let there be Peace.
Om Shanti, Shanti, Shanti.

ॐ

References

American Standard Bible
By AJ Holman Company

Critical Lives – Muhammad
By Yahiya Emerick

My Life and Quest
By Arthur Osborne

Ramana Marharshi and the Path of Self-Knowledge
By Arthur Osborne

The Essential Teachings of Ramana Maharshi
A Visual Journey
By Matthew Greenblat

The Teachings of Buddha
By Jack Kornfield

The Truth Is – *Sri H.W.L.*
by Prashanti de Jager

The Quickest Way to Enlightenment (Audio Tapes)
by The Gangji Foundation

The Holy Qur'an
By The Noor Foundation International
English Translation by Amatul Rahman Omar &
Abdul Mannan Omar

Timeless in Time – *Sri Bhagavan Ramana Maharshi*
A Biography by A. R. Natarajan